To our friend

JESTER HAIRSTON

*who taught people all over the world
to sing Negro spirituals
into world folk songs*

Contents

Understanding the Spirituals

People singing a Negro spiritual are often fascinated and puzzled at one and the same time by the words of the song. Their situation is like that of the Ethiopian secretary of the treasury described in the Book of Acts who, as he read Isaiah, was both intrigued and confused by what the prophet was saying. When Philip asked him, "Understandest thou what thou readest?" (Acts 8:30) the Ethiopian eagerly accepted help and began to discover unexpected and provocative dimensions of life and faith in the biblical text. Legend tells us that this politically powerful official came to have such a strong and radiant faith that he became the first missionary to Africa and there spread the good news of God in Jesus Christ to all his people.

The passage of Scripture which so perplexed him has also intrigued spiritual singers in every age: "He was led as a sheep to the slaughter; and like a lamb dumb before his shearer, so opened he not his mouth" (Isa. 53:7 as quoted in Acts 8:32). The Ethiopian inquired of Philip whether Isaiah was here speaking about himself or about someone else (Acts 8:34). Negro spirituals force us to ponder that same question when we come upon stanzas such as, "They nailed him to the tree/ An' he never said a mumbalin' word." People of every race and nation love to sing the best known spirituals. You, the reader, have a particular fondness for them I am sure.

I would like, therefore, to ask you, in the words of Philip: "Do you understand what you sing?" The life stories of these familiar—and even the not so familiar—spirituals are fascinating. We can follow them all the way from the King James Version of the Bible through the slavery period in the Old South to their present status as world folk songs of the late

twentieth century.   An explanation of even a few of the
spiritual texts opens up new and unexpected dimensions of
understanding about how God's Word can become incarnate,
take on flesh, in human—and inhuman—situations, even
today. We begin to see that the spirituals are as faith-engen-
dering and life-affirming for us in our time as they were for
the community of believers that originally created, shaped,
and preserved them. Old songs can be sung with new meaning, and new songs can be created so that the burdens which
weigh us down can be made lighter—as bearable as those of
the slaves who actually experienced freedom from their
chains while singing praise to him who has "the whole world
in his hands."

1.

Lit'le David

Lit'le David, play on yo' harp, Hallelu, hallelu
Lit'le David, play on yo' harp, Hallelu
Lit'le David, play on yo' harp, Hallelu, hallelu
Lit'le David, play on yo' harp, Hallelu.

1.
Lit'le David was a shepherd boy;
He killed Goliath an' shouted fo' joy.

2.
Joshua was de son of Nun;
He never would quit 'till his work
was done.

1.
Some come cripple and some come lame,
But dey went away walkin' in my God's name.

2.
Some come deaf and some come dumb,
But dey went away talkin' in my God's tongue.

"Lit'le David, play on yo' harp, Hallelu, hallelu" is an attractive, impelling chorus. It is so well done that it entices everybody to sing along in praise rather than to give up in despair.

Its positive attitude is sometimes contrasted with that of the people of Israel who, when deported into Babylonian captivity, hung their "harps upon the willows" and lamented: "They that carried us away captive required of us a song; and they that wasted us required of us mirth, saying, Sing us one of the songs of Zion. How shall we sing the Lord's song in a strange land?" (Ps. 137:2–4). Some interpreters have claimed that this ancient lamentation and the more recent spiritual songs of two enslaved peoples point to a difference between Jewish people and black people. There are segments of Judaism who to this day feel that they cannot sing songs of praise as long as the temple in Jerusalem has not been rebuilt; only lamenting is allowed in their synagogues, and in many of their worship services there is no music whatsoever: "How shall we sing the Lord's song in a strange land?"

1

The Babylonian captors obviously tried to make fun of the ancient Israelites' religion, treating their religious singing as hilarious entertainment. But the captives refused to have their faith thus defiled and ridiculed; they chose rather to yearn and long for Jerusalem where alone, they felt, true worship of their God could take place.

The Africans, who centuries later were carried away captive to a distant land, came from a quite different religious tradition, one which contributed immensely to their spiritual survival. For the African it was an accepted custom to subject oneself to the local deities whenever one entered a new territory; one obeyed, so to speak, the local "traffic rules." This basic structure of belief made it easier for those who, in the new land, first encountered the biblical God to gain a new identity as "children of the Lord." The ancestor religion and local tribal deities of Africa had been left behind. Moreover, family traditions could no longer be shared anyway because members of the same tribe and language were systematically separated from one another by the slave traders. The basic structure of belief remained, however, and was filled with new content.

The stories that were told and retold as good and bad examples for living were not those of blood relatives, but of faith relatives. The "strange land" in which the spirituals had their setting was neither Babylon, nor America, but earthly existence as such. "Home" was heaven—as experienced now in moments of liberating anticipation, and forever after death by all the faithful. Peter and Paul, Mary and Martha, Moses and David became ever-present companions on the pilgrimage through life.

The singers were not bothered by chronology, by the gap of two or three thousand years of history and development between the biblical era and their present. There was an immediacy about their relationship to biblical persons which allowed for intimacy in the midst of estrangement. We have to be careful not to project the feelings and understandings of our socially and religiously changed climate today into the social and religious climate of the eighteenth and nineteenth centuries.

Medieval Christian tradition, for example, had developed an elaborate understanding of saints, a system whereby the faithful could address believers of a bygone era and implore them to intercede with God to gain his favors. The spiritual singers, by contrast, never ask "Saint Paul" or "Saint Peter" or anybody else for intercession with God. They communicate with all the biblical characters on a basis of equality. They "talk" or even "chat" with them. The element of adoration, so important in mystical cults and some Christian traditions, is absent from the spirituals, which reflect instead a common existence in faith, a participatory devotion born of a sense of awareness, a confident feeling of belonging to the ever-present family of God.

For this reason the singer not only *tells about* David and Goliath, but actually *talks to* David; not, however, to "King" David, the greatest king, psalmist, and musician of Israel, but to "lit'le David." He can ask, command, encourage, or admonish biblical heroes as brothers.

The story of King Saul was well known. Whenever the moody and erratic king suffered severe depression, he would call for young David to play the harp and soothe his spirit (I Sam. 16:23). Yet this important service to a mighty master could be dangerous, for Saul was not always grateful for therapy; sometimes he would even throw his spear at the one who had done him so much good. With this background in mind the spiritual conveys a message of comfort and encouragement. The chorus, especially with its present imperative, "Lit'le David, *play* on yo' harp, Hallelu, hallelu," can have a marvelously uplifting impact on people who are in danger of succumbing to their depressions and harping on their frustrations instead of transforming their bitterness to praise.

Various lyrics have come to be associated with this chorus. The familiar couplet, "Lit'le David was a shepherd boy; / He killed Goliath an' shouted fo' joy," summarizes a biblical narrative which has encouraged believers down through the

ages who felt hopelessly disadvantaged in the face of powerful opponents or overwhelming odds. The shepherd boy
David, with a mere slingshot, had killed the heavily armored
Philistine giant who had been mocking the God of Israel and
bragging that he would destroy God's people (1 Sam. 17).

The second stanza, which actually derives from a different
spiritual, sings about another favorite Old Testament hero,
Joshua. The successor of Moses is mentioned, however, not
because he successfully besieged fortified Jericho with trumpets and shouts, but as an example of endurance and de-
pendability at the battle of Ajalon: "Joshua was de son of
Nun; / He never would quit 'till his work was done." In
most spirituals about the battle of Ajalon (Josh. 10:12–14)
the emphasis is on God's stopping the sun, or on Joshua's
effective prayer, but in one version the lesson is drawn that
the sun won't stop for you so "nebber let it katch-er you wid
yo' work undone." "Joshua was de son of Nun" (Josh. 1:1)
supplied the necessary rhyme for "work un*done*," but the
phrase also carried special significance for the singers, who
often knew neither of their parents. Slaves readily admitted,
"Sometimes I feel like a motherless chile"—a child of *none*.
It was uplifting to realize that God could use even orphaned
people for his mighty deeds. Even a nobody in the eyes of
man was somebody in God's eyes, and this was added reason
to sing "Hallelu" instead of lamenting.

Another version of the "Lit'le David" spiritual adds two
New Testament references which give it a very different
function:

> Some come cripple and some come lame,
> But dey went away walkin' in my God's name.
>
> Some come deaf and some come dumb,
> But dey went away talkin' in my God's tongue.

When John the Baptist, herald of Jesus, was imprisoned by
Herod and wondered whether or not his whole ministry of
preaching and baptizing would be in vain, he sent some of his
friends to Jesus in order to find out whether this wandering

preacher actually was the expected Messiah. Ever since King David's time the hope had been kept alive that a new king of Israel would come and establish an everlasting kingdom of peace. Isaiah had prophesied about the Day of the Lord:

> Say to them that are of a fearful heart, Be strong, fear not: behold, your God will come with vengeance, even God with a recompense; he will come and save you. Then the eyes of the blind shall be opened, and the ears of the deaf shall be unstopped. Then shall the lame man leap as a hart, and the tongue of the dumb sing. (Isa. 35:4—6)

Jesus referred to this prophecy—though not to the vengeance part—when he answered the friends of John: "The blind receive their sight, and the lame walk, the lepers are cleansed, and the deaf hear, the dead are raised up, and the poor have the gospel preached to them" (Matt. 11:5).

So also the spiritual singer recalls the same words: the prophecy is fulfilled, the Day of the Lord has appeared in Jesus Christ; he is the expected son of David who brings divine peace to the whole world. The singer feels himself a part of this miraculous new dimension of life, for he says that those who have been healed "went away walkin' in *my* God's name," "went away talkin' in *my* God's tongue." The gospel has been preached to the singer himself and he too has received a new language of praise.

For the believer it makes sense to ask all "lit'le Davids" everywhere to "play on yo' harp" and to sing and play "hallelu" in any "strange land," in all times and circumstances, because "my God" has been experienced as the one who fulfills all hopes and relativizes all problems. Healthy, meaningful survival becomes an option for all of us under any and all conditions, even where others want to "waste us away" (Ps. 137:3). Instead of wasting ourselves away by harping on our problems and griping about our depressions, we can redirect our feelings to wholesome praise. We can "walk in God's name" out of the crippling grip of the enemies that frustrate and destroy our lives. We can also discern God's word of love sounding in, through, above, and despite the deafening noises of complaint and revenge, becoming vocal within ourselves and active for justice. We can even find ourselves "talking in God's tongue," just as Jesus in his compassion walked and talked and lived for the outcasts of his time.

2.

Kum Ba Yah, My Lord

1.
Kum ba yah, my Lord, Kum ba yah!
Kum ba yah, my Lord, Kum ba yah!
Kum ba yah, my Lord, Kum ba yah!
Oh, Lord, Kum ba yah.

2.
Someone's crying, Lord, Kum ba yah!
Someone's crying, Lord, Kum ba yah!
Someone's crying, Lord, Kum ba yah!
Oh, Lord, Kum ba yah.

3.
Someone's singing, Lord, Kum ba yah!
Someone's singing, Lord, Kum ba yah!
Someone's singing, Lord, Kum ba yah!
Oh, Lord, Kum ba yah.

4.
Someone's praying, Lord, Kum ba yah!
Someone's praying, Lord, Kum ba yah!
Someone's praying, Lord, Kum ba yah!
Oh, Lord, Kum ba yah.

This quiet, beautiful song is said to have made many a long journey. Born among deported Africans in America, perhaps as a prayer request, "Come by here, my Lord, come by here!" it was carried back to Africa by freed slaves returning to the continent from whence they had come. There it was discovered later by American missionaries who brought it back to the United States. Sometimes it is ascribed to Liberia, sometimes to Angola. Sometimes it is called a Negro spiritual, sometimes an American spiritual. It should be called a "world spiritual," for it has made many journeys across the ocean and is sung all over the world, wherever people ask for God's presence because "someone's crying" or "someone's praying."

During the past decade new and highly contemporary lines were added:

> Churches are burning, Lord . . .
> Somebody's starving, Lord . . .
> Somebody's shooting, Lord . . .
> We want justice, Lord . . .
> We want freedom, Lord, come by here!

7

But people like to invite their Lord also to happy occasions: "Someone's singing, Lord, Kum ba yah!" Adapted slightly, the song can be used in lieu of the widely known dinner blessing: "Come, Lord Jesus, here, be our guest." The song can easily be adapted and extended since only one word of the basic outline has to be changed in order to add another stanza.

This prayer-song is as simple and consoling as a lullaby. People everywhere need such comfort and consolation. We all share the experience of needing God's loving presence in the midst of our daily routines and concerns. Our whole being responds when the spiritual concludes with its universal sigh for relief and love, "Oh, Lord, Kum ba yah!"

3.

Oh! Didn't It Rain

Oh! didn't it rain, Oh! didn't it rain,
Oh! didn't it rain, Oh! didn't it rain,
Some forty days and nights.

1.
They called old Noah a foolish man
Oh! didn't it rain.
Cause Noah build de ark upon dry land.
Oh! didn't it rain.

2.
When it begun to rain,
Oh! didn't it rain.
Women and children begun to scream.
Oh! didn't it rain.

3.
It rain all day and it rain all night,
Oh! didn't it rain.
It rain 'til mountain top was out of sight.
Oh! didn't it rain.

4.
God told Noah by the rainbow sign:
Oh! didn't it rain.
No more water but fire next time.
Oh! didn't it rain.

5.
Judgment Day is coming,
Coming in the Prophet's way.
Some folks say they never prayed
    a prayer;
They sho' will pray that day.

"God told Noah" something more than what the fourth stanza of this song would lead us to believe. Its rhyming couplet appears in many different spirituals. In this song the lines appear in the context of the Flood narrative, a past judgment day which is considered little more than a mild warning in comparison to the devastating Judgment Day to come.

Perhaps because extremely heavy rains and floodings have always been a terrifying reality for everyone living along a big river—but especially for people housed in slave shanties on the bank—a number of spirituals make reference to the great Flood. Mahalia Jackson is remembered for her singing

"O didn't it, didn't it, didn't it rain,/ Rain, rain, rain, children, didn't it rain." There are spirituals about the "old ark" which perfectly simulate the rhythm of the "moverin' " along on the ripples of the river, or express the dangers when "the old ark she reel, the old ark she rock."

Our goal here is not to compare all the vivid images growing out of the Noah story, but to observe for a moment the evolution of spiritual texts with a few interesting "specimens" or "fossils" characteristic of different stages in the development of the song. In the last stage, the last piece to be broken off has been used as the title of the famous book, *The Fire Next Time*. The very title of James Baldwin's bestseller has caused chills of excitement and fear to run through the bodies of millions both here and abroad. The singers' simple prediction has indeed come a long way. It is really the isolated final part of one of these "wandering couplets" which, over the course of time, has become independent of its context and is now sung wherever it fits rhythmically or wherever people want to sing one more stanza or feel that a warning from God is needed.

> God told Noah by the rainbow sign:
> No more water but fire next time.

This couplet had a history of its own. An earlier formulation reads: "Gawd give Noah de rainbow sign, / He tol' him no mo' watuh but fiah nex' time." But the two lines here were unbalanced, the second being too long and busy. It was an improvement when, in another version, "He tol' him" was simply dropped. But then the two statements were unconnected and incomplete. They finally began to make sense when, in a third version, "Gawd give de" was replaced by "God told 'bout de," although the abbreviated form of "about" was not yet smooth and this problem remained unsolved until "by" replaced " 'bout": "God told Noah by the rainbow sign: / No more water but fire next time." Now in this most popular version, both lines consist of seven short words rhythmically well balanced and rhyming at the end.

The message is clear and packed as concisely and simply as possible. The rainbow sign has become a kind of visual aid by which God teaches his lesson about an even harsher punishment. Much later, indeed only in our time, the couplet was truncated to make the last quarter stand alone as an ominous warning from the alienated and angry: "fire next time."

The earliest phases of this textual evolution are not documented. The preacher to whom the singing congregation responded might have been responsible for taking an isolated New Testament text and recasting it in the time frame of Noah and the Flood (Gen. 6–9). The Flood is documented in several ancient religious traditions. The biblical writers interpret it to mean that God tried to clean out all wickedness from among the people by sending these terrible rains. God preserved none except righteous Noah and his family, in an ark, but then, when everything was over, even Noah and his family sinned and God came to the sad realization that this all-out method of purification had not accomplished his goal. Therefore God promised: "Neither shall all flesh be cut off any more by the waters of a flood; neither shall there any more be a flood to destroy the earth. I do set my bow in the cloud, and it shall be for a token of a covenant between me and the earth" (Gen. 9:11, 13).

For a society of nomads and hunters God's promise offered a marvelous consolation! God had hung his fierce bow in the clouds as a dependable token that the hostilities between heaven and earth were over, that a covenant for the sustenance of life had been made and the gulf of fear and enmity was bridged. It was a beautiful explanation of this marvelous, colorful arch which connects earth and sky after a horrifying, devastating thunderstorm. The rainbow became a symbol for the everlasting love and goodness of a God who, while he could get irritated and angry about the sinfulness of man and would indeed punish sinners, firmly pledges that he will never exterminate all of mankind. For the singer the "rainbow sign" became a technical term for this God-given

pledge that there would be "no more water," never again a
universal flood, no all-consuming catastrophe.

One Gospel writer records Jesus' reference to Noah: "As
it was in the days of Noe, so shall it be also in the days of the
Son of man" (Luke 17:26). His point was that people over-
look the warning signs and do not prepare themselves for
God's kingdom; instead they live merrily on until they get
caught by surprise.

Jesus exemplified the suddenness with which the kingdom
of God will come by referring to yet another well-known
horror story. People at Lot's time went about their corrupt
business and exploitive pleasures as if everything were safe
and sound, solid and secure. They would not listen to any
warning signals, and did not want to be reminded of how
they were totally disregarding God's covenant. "But the
same day that Lot went out of Sodom it rained fire and brim-
stone from heaven, and destroyed them all" (Luke 17:29).

The same examples were used by the author of 2 Peter,
who wrote to "stir up your pure minds" (3:1). But this New
Testament writer reinterpreted the meaning of the Flood.
He dropped God's promise, symbolized by the rainbow, never
to destroy mankind by flood again, and saw the Flood as a
mild punishment foreshadowing the far more horrible destruction of the whole cosmos at the "day of judgment and
perdition of ungodly men . . . wherein the heavens being on
fire shall be dissolved and the elements shall melt with fer-
vent heat" (2 Pet. 3:7, 12). This third chapter of 2 Peter,
which also expresses the confident expectation of a promised
"new heavens and a new earth, wherein dwelleth righteousness" (3:13), caught the imagination of many believers ex-
pecting the end time. We hear of "elements meltin' " and
the "world on fire" also in many Negro spirituals referring
to the Last Judgment.

These spirituals are a beautiful example of how singers
selected vivid images from abstract biblical passages in order
to create dramatic scenes with which the people could easily
identify. In our couplet about Noah "the rainbow sign,"

which was God's cosmic guarantee for *mercy* in the Bible, has become the reminder of impending *punishment*. With this reversed meaning the couplet was handed down in song from generation to generation. It is not surprising that the angry and alienated of our day adopted the phrase as a powerful slogan, a threat that they themselves would fulfill God's prophecy by setting the cities on fire if social conditions were not improved and justice established. Their hope was for a "world of righteousness" after the old world of sin and oppression had melted away.

Many famous contemporary authors warn of man's technological capacity for triggering self-made catastrophies. They fear that humans are actually capable of ending life on this earth in ways more horrible than the writers of Revelation and 2 Peter ever imagined. What these modern prophets of doom usually lack, however, is the counterbalancing vision of a glorious new heaven and earth promised by a merciful God to whom people can turn in their moment of deepest distress. As the spiritual singer puts it: "They sho' will pray that day."

4.

Jacob's Ladder

1.
We are climbing Jacob's ladder,
We are climbing Jacob's ladder,
We are climbing Jacob's ladder,
Soldiers of the cross.

2.
Ev'ry round goes higher 'n' higher,
Ev'ry round goes higher 'n' higher,
Ev'ry round goes higher 'n' higher,
Soldiers of the cross.

3.
Brother, do you love my Jesus,
Brother, do you love my Jesus,
Brother, do you love my Jesus,
Soldiers of the cross.

4.
If you love him why not serve him,
If you love him why not serve him,
If you love him why not serve him,
Soldiers of the cross.

If John Bunyan had written his religious bestseller *The Pilgrim's Progress* in the American South, he could easily have incorporated many a spiritual: "I hear dem angels calling loud, / Keep in de middle ob de road"; "Keep inching along like a poor inchworm"; "Don't let it be said too late." Life, in many of the spirituals, is perceived as a troublesome journey on the narrow road through valleys and over mountaintops to the pearly gates of heaven. As it was, Bunyan wrote earlier, in seventeenth-century England. His book and the Bible were often the only "library" the early settlers brought with them to the new country. Having left their homeland for reasons of faith, many Christian families used both books regularly for devotional reading and for guidance in daily living. Indeed, *Pilgrim's Progress* and the Bible were the main sources of outside stimulation and entertainment before radio, magazines, movies, and television took over. It is highly probable that the dramatic struggle of Bunyan's hero, "Christian," with all the problems and temptations of life as he made his way along the "narrow road" up to the "pearly

gates" and on into the "golden streets" of heaven, inspired
many a house slave to take courage for his or her own difficult journey through life, and to respond with singing.

The spirituals have a variety of biblical images about how
a pilgrim gets into heaven. Some sing about walking to and
through a gate, others about crossing over Jordan. Jacob's
ladder provided yet another image for getting from here to
there.

Jacob's dream at the pagan sanctuary of Bethel has excited
the imagination of artists throughout the ages. At the time
of the vision, Jacob was a scared, hunted, homeless fugitive.
He was fleeing from his brother Esau who was furious because Jacob had cheated him out of his birthright, his property. Weary of his journey, indeed dead-tired, Jacob lay
down and fell asleep—and there at Bethel experienced a
dream which changed his entire life. In the ancient world
dreams were accepted as legitimate and even common means
for God to appear to humans and reveal his will to them.
The Old Testament dreams of Joseph in Egypt, or the New
Testament dreams of Joseph the father of Jesus, for instance,
were by no means "merely a dream," something unreal to
be wiped away by washing one's face in the morning. On
the contrary, they were divine revelation, and their commands had to be obeyed; their threats and promises would
surely be fulfilled, so men had better heed them! In his
dream-vision at Bethel, Jacob saw a ladder reaching all the
way from earth to heaven with angels descending and
ascending:

> The Lord stood above it, and said, I am the Lord God of
> Abraham thy father, and the God of Isaac: the land whereon
> thou liest, to thee will I give it, and to thy seed; And thy
> seed shall be as the dust of the earth; and thou shalt spread
> abroad . . . and in thee and in thy seed shall all the families
> of the earth be blessed. And, behold, I am with thee, and
> will keep thee in all places whither thou goest.
>
> (Gen. 28:13–15)

It is amazing that the homeless, landless slaves who were

cut off from their clan in Africa and lost their children on the auction-block in America did not latch on with great fascination and consolation to this reaffirmation of God's promise to Abraham, to grant land along with countless descendants. In the universalized Christian tradition, however, which referred the hints and hopes of the "promised land" more to heaven than to real estate, the emphasis of Jacob's vision shifted. Whereas in the biblical story the ladder was only a visual aid for reintroducing the all-important promise of land and descendants—it meant survival as a people blessed of God—in post-biblical songs and spirituals the ladder itself took on a central position. It was seen as a means of communication between humans and God, indeed as a miraculous way of getting into heaven, where all earthly worries will be over.

A popular belief growing out of this vision in Europe included the concept of cute guardian angels. The concept was widely popularized by Humperdink's opera "Hansel and Gretel" in which fourteen pretty angels descend from heaven and guard the forlorn children as they sing "Now I lay me down to sleep. . . ." A picture of this sentimental scene, or some variation of it, hung over many a child's bed before Walt Disney's time: beautiful angels guiding and leading the innocent passive soul up to heaven.

Interestingly enough, where the spirituals sing of Jacob's ladder the angels play no role whatsoever. The spirituals stress the personal initiative, determination, and effort of the believer: "I'm goin' to climb up Jacob's ladder," "I want to climb up Jacob's ladder," "Want to go to hebben when I die . . . Jacob's ladder deep an' long. . . ." Indeed, this last version comes close to the river image for death: "Jordan's river deep and wide" or "chilly and cold." The ladder, like the river, represents the last obstacle to be overcome before the faithful can arrive in the heavenly home and finally relax, freed from all of their burdens. In the spirituals there are no angelic helpers because the experience of God's presence "in all places whither thou goest" is enough.

The best-known song about the dream-vision, however, has a slightly different perspective. Here, all of life is like the ascending ladder. "We are climbing Jacob's ladder," not at the end of our horizontal journey, where at death we would have to climb straight up into heaven, but rather throughout our entire life. All of life involves a steady movement upward: "Ev'ry round goes higher 'n' higher." What the spiritual expresses is perceivable progress towards the fulfillment of our earthly destiny.

The concluding line of each stanza, "Soldiers of the cross," reminds us not only of the "exceeding great army" which the "dry bones" formed after their resurrection in Ezekiel's vision (Ezek. 37:10), but also of another favorite image which recurs prominently in old hymns like "Onward Christian Soldiers." As "soldiers of the cross" Christians should not become weary in conquering sin and evil, but persevere even in hardships until life's victory is won.

The army of the Lord knows no discrimination. Even the blind and the lame may join and be victorious "when de saints come marchin' in." The stanzas are often multiplied: not only the "brother," but also the "sister" and the "elder" and the "sinner" are asked whether they "love my Jesus," which is the only entrance requirement: "No man cometh unto the Father, but by me" (John 14:6). There are no physical, racial, social, economic, or political characteristics which could disqualify a person. The only standard for qualification is the spiritual criterion: love of Jesus. In this army, service to the commander is based on a relationship of love and commitment: "If you love him, why not serve him!"

The military images of the spirituals and hymns, like those of the Bible—for instance, "put on the whole armor of God . . . (Eph. 6:11)—stem from a time when being a soldier was unquestionably the highest accomplishment and honor for a young man. In evaluating such images we must be careful not to project contemporary post-Vietnam feelings about war and the military into these texts. The notion that Christians are "soldiers of the cross" was meant to relativize the abso-

lute claims of any human commander and to make love the
supreme command, and unwavering obedience to its dictates
the highest form of commitment and service. It follows quite
logically, therefore, that other versions of "Jacob's Ladder"
have as a chorus a quote from a hymn praising God as Lord:

> I will praise ye de Lawd;
> I will praise him till I die,
> I will praise him till I die,
> In de new Jerusalem.

or:

> O praise ye the Lord;
> I'll praise him till I die,
> I'll praise him till I die,
> And sing Jerusalem.

The believer is a soldier in the army of the "Lord, the
Almighty." The command to praise—rather than to complain to—the Lord, which appears in numerous psalms and
has been incorporated into many church hymns such as
"Praise ye the Lord, the Almighty, the King of Creation,"
also found its way into spiritual choruses. However, the King
James phrase "praise ye the Lord"—which uses *ye,* the older
form for *you*—was seen simply as an independent unit of
elevated praise which could be used anywhere without concern for grammar. "I will praise ye de Lawd" was the
spiritual singer's way of celebrating praise as the lifelong and
irrevocable commitment of a "soldier of the cross" who
looked forward at the end, not to a medal of honor but to
unbounded gladness and continuing praise in his marvelous
new home, the heavenly Jerusalem.

5.

Swing Low, Sweet Chariot

Swing low, sweet chariot,
Coming for to carry me home;
Swing low, sweet chariot,
Coming for to carry me home.

1.

I looked over Jordan and what did I see,
Coming for to carry me home?
A band of angels coming after me,
Coming for to carry me home.

2.

If you get there before I do,
Coming for to carry me home,
Tell all my friends I'm coming too,
Coming for to carry me home.

3.

I'm sometimes up, I'm sometimes down,
Coming for to carry me home,
But still my soul feels heavenly bound,
Coming for to carry me home.

"Swing low, sweet chariot" strikes a responsive chord in all of us. It helps transform our fears of death into an expectant hope born of faith. The song recalls two extraordinary biblical episodes, the story of Elijah in the Old Testament and the parable of the rich man and Lazarus in the New Testament. In the Old Testament the prophet Elijah was walking with his friend and student, Elisha, by the Jordan River when "there appeared a chariot of fire, and horses of fire, and parted them both asunder; and Elijah went up by a whirlwind into heaven" (2 Kings 2:11). In the New Testament Jesus told a parable about a rich man whom tradition calls Dives—the Latin adjective for rich—and a poor beggar, Lazarus, who died "and was carried by the angels into Abraham's bosom" (Luke 16:22).

History, geography, and sermon fuse into a visionary landscape for dying believers. The faithful see the Jordan as a dividing boundary between the here and the beyond. Some songs describe it as a "deep and wide" or a "chilly and cold" river which believers yearn somehow to "cross over." Some

of the faithful ask the archangel Michael (Dan. 12:1–7) to
"row the boat ashore." Others encourage the stream itself to
"roll up, Jordan, roll up high" so that they might walk
through on dry ground, as did Elijah and Elisha (2 Kings
2:8) or, more probably, as did Joshua and the children of
Israel when they finally crossed over into the Promised Land
(Josh. 3:13–17). Again, others request Elijah's chariot to
carry them across.

In "Swing Low," however, the awe-inspiring, even terrifying fire of the chariot, the horses, and also the frightening
whirlwind of the Old Testament story have not become a
part of the poetic vision. Instead, the believer calls for the
"sweet" chariot to swing down low, so that he can enter for
his journey home to heaven. The whirlwind of the Elijah
story is replaced by more personal messengers of God, the
angels from the Lazarus story. The believer envisions a
whole "band of angels" coming specifically for him. A gospel-
song version even set their number at twenty-four. The number seems to come from John's vision: "I saw four and twenty
elders sitting, clothed in white raiment; and they had on
their heads crowns of gold" (Rev. 4:4). The singer, unable
to believe that such a high honor would be extended to him,
expresses humble amazement: "And what did I see?" In his
humility, however, he also senses a deep satisfaction; having
probably never been honored in his lifetime, he is now
receiving the most beautiful, trouble-free "welcome home"
after a most difficult, trouble-filled journey here on earth.
Johann Sebastian Bach was another believer who could justly
call the chariot "sweet"; he entitled one of his most moving
arias "Come Sweet Death."

"Swing Low" is such a beautiful song that people don't
like to stop with just one stanza about the angels' coming
across Jordan to extend a welcome. It is easy for a good song
leader to add two more short solo lines and have the group
join in to repeat the familiar alternate line, "Coming for to
carry me home." The rhyming couplet "If you get there
before I do, / Tell all my friends I'm coming too" provides

such an additional stanza, one that is sung in various spirit-uals about the journey to heaven where the great reunion of friends and loved ones will take place.

"I'm sometimes up, I'm sometimes down, / But still my soul feels heavenly bound" is another wandering couplet which is easy to remember and fits well into many different choruses. The stanza seems to belong to the chorus "Nobody Knows the Trouble I've Seen." In that context it is known as "Sometimes I'm up, sometimes I'm down, O yes, Lord, / Sometimes I'm almost to the ground, O yes, Lord." A couplet that poignantly expresses a feeling which overcomes all of us so often in so many different circumstances cannot pos-sibly "belong" to only one song; it may be sung and varied whenever a singer feels like it. "Down" rhymes as well with "groun' " as it does with "boun'." But the singer of "Nobody Knows" is so downcast and desperately lonely that he has almost lost sight of the vision of "home" and the friends awaiting him there. This second line almost grounds him on the "down." By contrast, the second line of the couplet in "Swing Low" helps the believer who has a "low" to swing out of it and up; his soul still feels "heavenly bound," ori-ented toward God despite the ups and downs of life's journey.

6.

Go Down, Moses

Go down, Moses,
'Way down in Egypt land,
Tell ol' Pharaoh,
Let my people go!

1.
When Israel was in Egypt's land,
  Let my people go.
Oppressed so hard they could not stand,
  Let my people go.

2.
Thus said the Lord, bold Moses said, . . .
If not I'll smite your firstborn dead. . . .

3.
No more shall they in bondage toil; . . .
Let them come out with Egypt's spoil. . . .

4.
When Israel out of Egypt came . . .
And left the proud oppressive land, . . .

5.
O, 'twas a dark and dismal night . . .
When Moses led the Israelites. . . .

6.
'Twas good ole Moses and Aaron, too, . . .
'Twas they that led the armies through. . . .

7.
The Lord told Moses what to do . . .
To lead the children of Israel through. . . .

8.
O come along, Moses, you'll not get lost; . . .
Stretch out your rod and come across. . . .

9.
As Israel stood by the water side, . . .
At the command of God it did divide. . . .

10.
When they had reached the other shore . . .
They sang a song of triumph o'er. . . .

11.
Pharaoh said he would go across, . . .
But Pharaoh and his host were lost. . . .

12.
O, Moses, the cloud shall cleave the way, . . .
A fire by night, a shade by day. . . .
13.
You'll not get lost in the wilderness . . .
With a lighted candle in your breast. . . .

14.
Jordan shall stand up like a wall, . . .
And the walls of Jericho shall fall. . . .

15.
Your foes shall not before you stand, . . .
And you'll possess fair Canaan's land. . . .

16.
'Twas just about at harvest time . . .
When Joshua led his host divine. . . .

17.
O let us all from bondage flee . . .
And let us all in Christ be free. . . .

18.
We need not always weep and moan . . .
And wear these slavery chains forlorn. . . .

19.
This world's a wilderness of woe; . . .
O, let us on to Canaan go. . . .

20.
What a beautiful morning that will be . . .
When time breaks up in eternity. . . .

21.
O brethren, brethren, you'd better
   be engaged, . . .
For the devil he's out on a big
   rampage. . . .

22.
The devil he thought he had
   me fast, . . .
But I thought I'd break his chains
   at last. . . .

23.
O take yer shoes from off your feet . . .
And walk into the golden street. . . .

24.
I'll tell you what I likes de best: . . .
It is the shouting Methodist. . . .

25.
I do believe without a doubt . . .
That a Christian has the right to shout. . . .

This well-known spiritual has often been regarded primarily as a code song, that is, a song which not only expressed a yearning for deliverance from Southern slavery but also signaled the moment for action to achieve it. Other interpreters disregard this revolutionary possibility altogether. It is the plot itself, not the lyrics as such, that causes this double perspective. It was not only the successful exodus of Moses and the children of Israel from Egyptian slavery but also "lit'le David's" victory over the giant Goliath that has inspired suffering people ever since. Through all of Judeo-Christian history, powerless individuals and groups have identified with the victorious underdog and gained vicarious satisfaction in the horrifying punishments which plagued Pharaoh and in the humiliating death of the bragging Goliath. During the Third Reich, for instance, when the pastor preached about David and Goliath, the underground church understood that in that one-sided contest Goliath represented Hitler, and that God would now stand by his small band of weak, outnumbered, and mocked Confessing Christians even as he had stood by and supported David. A Gestapo spy, however, hearing the very same sermon could not—even if he got the message—denounce the pastor as subversive, so long as the sermon stayed within the terminology and framework of the biblical story.

A secret code of this sort functions effectively in public only when its normal surface meaning hides the special significance it holds for the initiated. Frederick Douglass, a famous insurgent slave, reportedly used a popular religious song of the time, "O Canaan, sweet Canaan, I am bound for the land of Canaan," as a signal for concrete action.

Jesus refused to seek or wield political power, to be crowned king, or to free his people from Roman oppression through violence. Nevertheless, for the New Testament writers Jesus was greater than Moses and David—who had freed and ruled the kingdom of Israel without shrinking from violence—because his nonviolent love frees all the peoples of the earth from the oppression of sin and leads them into the "promised land" of God's ultimate kingdom. Interestingly enough, sermon applications of the long and detailed biblical accounts of Moses and David have oscillated between spiritual and political interpretations ever since.

"Go Down, Moses" shared this oscillation in the course of its development. It includes the central idea of the Exodus—that because God acted mightily and miraculously in the past, believers may be assured of his mighty hand today to free them from unjust political oppression. At the same time the song also breathes the hope of a spiritual freedom from the oppression of sin. The two interpretations are not mutually exclusive. Their combination, however, is peculiarly American. Many white Protestants, who had escaped hardship and persecution in Europe, believed fervently that free America was the promised land; and yet they too yearned for and sang about ultimate freedom in Canaan, the Promised Land, and of heaven with God. The two concepts were simply not opposed to each other in early America as they tend to be today.

Biblical scholarship has shown that many an ancient story or writing has been attributed to a well-known personality in order to give that writing greater credence and weight. Such attribution has also occurred with respect to the spiritual "Go Down, Moses," which is often ascribed to Harriet Tubman. She was a true heroine in the "underground railroad," a network of courageous people stretching all the way from the South to the North and beyond into Canada, whose concern was to help slaves escape to freedom. "General Tubman," as she was called, helped several hundred of her people escape from slavery and reach the "promised land" of the free North. She surely deserved the honorary title "Moses," by which she was also known. Yet the spiritual is greater than any particular historic personage or episode and has served to inspire courage and faith in people all over the world whose freedom was at stake.

As always, and especially where different theories of interpretation are involved, it is worthwhile to look at the text itself. The Bible devotes many chapters to describing how the children of Israel dwelling in Egypt suffered under the slave labor which was imposed on them ever more harshly by Pharaoh. As time went on he demanded longer working hours and greater output while cutting their supplies of raw material and food. He even commanded the killing of all male infants in the slave families. It is truly amazing that the slave songs referring to the Exodus hardly mention the suffering of the Israelite slaves even though the singers had witnessed and experienced slave treatment themselves and could have found in the Israelites' suffering a perfectly acceptable vehicle for complaint and lament about their own suffering. The biblical account also details the gory plagues, which Moses interpreted as God's punishment upon the oppressors. Ten horrible catastrophes befell the Egyptians. Their harvest was destroyed by grasshoppers, their land overrun by frogs, their water turned to blood, their firstborn slain. Here was ample material to excite the imagination of any person looking for revenge for injustices. The writers of the Book of Exodus and of many of the Psalms obviously rejoice in the deserved punishments inflicted upon their oppressors. They even ask God for the most horrible revenge on their enemies, including women and children (cf. Ps. 137:8–9). Yet there is nothing of this vengeful desire in the dominant tradition of the spirituals. They are an admirable testimony to a forgiving faith whose human greatness cannot be overestimated.

Modern song books are primarily interested in short, singable songs. As a result, older songs—which were often long and involved sermons—appear with only a select few of their more popular stanzas intact. The truncation obviously gives a distorted image of the song's original meaning and function. "Go Down, Moses," for example, has recently become a chorus of liberation involving only one or two stanzas of more or less related wandering couplets, whereas at one time it was a long narrative song. The Jubilee Singers recorded twenty-five stanzas. This group, the first black choir to tour the United States and abroad, made the slave songs not only "acceptable" but famous. The choir was made up of Fisk University students, "learned" folks who could remember well old song traditions and who had input from various singing communities out of which they selected the material to form their own version.

Other Exodus songs are shorter and simpler in style and vocabulary. The old "Hammer Song," for example, was sung at work to the rhythm of the hammering, each blow driving home the message more forcefully. It offers an interesting comparison to "Go Down, Moses."

> Don't you hear God talking?   [hammering]
> He's talking to Moses.   [hammering]
> He's talking through thunder.   [hammering]
> God tol' Moses: [hammering]
> Go down in Egyp',   [hammering]
> Go tell ol' Pharaoh   [hammering]
> To loose his people.   [hammering]
> Ol' Pharaoh had a hard heart   [hammering]
> An' would not loose dem.   [hammering]

Exodus 4:21 had the Lord say: "But I will harden his heart, that he shall not let the people go." The "Hammer Song" characterizing Pharaoh as a man with a "hard heart," suggests that evil is rooted in the character of people. The spirituals do not indulge in theological and philosophical speculations on the age-old problem of theodicy, the ultimate cause or source of evil. They hold simply that God commands the right thing, but sinners refuse to obey.

The middle lines of the old "Hammer Song" were smoothed out in logic and in style when "to loose *his* people" was replaced in the chorus of "Go Down, Moses" by the direct biblical quotation: "Thus saith the Lord God of Israel, Let *my* people go" (Exod. 5:1). The second stanza of the Jubilee version begins: "Thus said the Lord, bold Moses said, Let my people go!" From this context the imperative became the refrain for all the stanzas, with the repeated chorus after each stanza hammering the threatening theme into the memories of all "ol' Pharaohs."

The final line of stanza 2, "If not I'll smite your firstborn dead," offers the only alternative to obedience, namely, the last and harshest of the ten plagues. "If thou refuse to let him go, behold, I will slay thy son, even thy firstborn" (Exod. 4:23) is the only plague mentioned in the song. The Bible reports the execution of the threat and the institution of the Passover, neither of which was of interest to the singers.

Only one line in the twenty-five stanzas sketches the slavery situation, which had become unbearable: "oppressed so hard they could not stand." "Ye shall spoil the Egyptians" (Exod. 3:22), God's command to the oppressed, was reformulated as a message to Pharaoh: "No more shall they in bondage toil; / Let them come out with Egypt's spoil." However, the spiritual does not elaborate on the clever and lucrative spoiling of the Egyptians by the Israelites, which could have offered such rich material for a vengeful mind.

We must conclude from our textual analysis that a spirit of hate and resentment was not present in the spirituals. Some interpreters today project into the slaves feelings such as we would probably have felt if we were to find ourselves in a similar situation, but this is not the same as a historical statement of how it actually was. Many slaves had learned, with Paul, to rejoice in whatever state or condition they were in (Rom. 12:12, 14; Phil. 4:11) as well as to be ready to improve their condition when possible: "Art thou called being a servant? care not for it: but if thou mayest be made free, use it rather" (1 Cor. 7:21).

The first three stanzas of "Go Down, Moses" are about the only ones known today; however, they are merely the introduction to the story of the people's long way through the wilderness to the Promised Land. Thus, in the form in which the song is best known one hears only of the threatening demand for freedom. The hard struggle experienced in living out that freedom in the wilderness, which takes up many chapters in the Bible and many stanzas in the fuller text of the song, is forgotten.

The Exodus itself is factually stated in stanza 4 by quoting the first two lines of the hymn "Omnipotence and Immutability":

> When Israel out of Egypt came
> And left the proud oppressor's land,
> Supported by the great I Am,
> Safe in the hollow of his hand,
> The Lord of Israel reigned alone
> And Judah was his fav'rite throne.

In the spiritual, however, the hymn-sentence is left incomplete, without all the complicated abstruse words that follow. The main interest of the spiritual, according to the Jubilee version, has to do with the marching to the Promised Land and overcoming the many obstacles along the way in the wilderness, or even better, with the singers' own pilgrimage to the promised heavenly land and their overcoming the various obstacles in life. The bard utilizes the past tense to summarize the events recorded in the Book of Exodus but switches from the position of the human narrator to the direct speech of God in stanza 8 when he visualizes bold Moses as one of the "children" in difficulty needing encouragement. "O come along, Moses, you'll not get lost; / Stretch out your rod and come across." The biblical account reads:

And the Lord said unto Moses, Wherefore criest thou unto me? speak unto the children of Israel, that they go forward: But lift thou up thy rod, and stretch out thine hand over the sea, and divide it: and the children of Israel shall go on dry ground through the midst of the sea . . . and the Lord caused the sea to go back by a strong east wind all that night, and made the sea dry land, and the waters were divided. And the children of Israel went into the midst of the sea upon the dry ground: and the waters were a wall unto them on their right hand, and on their left.

(Exod. 14:15–16, 21–22)

Accordingly, the singer summarizes in stanza 9: "As Israel stood by the water side, / At the command of God it did divide," but in stanza 14 he uses the image of the passage through the Red Sea for a promise of safe and dry passage through the river Jordan as well: "Jordan shall stand up like a wall" (cf. Josh. 3:15–17). Since in the spirituals "Jordan" refers mostly to the dividing line between wilderness-like earthly life and promised heavenly life, this crossing over became a metaphor for a good death, a transition eased by a concerned God. The oscillation between historical account and metaphorical interpretation becomes very obvious: "You'll not get lost in the wilderness / With a lighted candle in your breast" (13). The external light of the Exodus experience—"The Lord went before them by day in a pillar of a cloud, to lead them the way; and by night in a pillar of fire, to give them light; to go by day and night" (Exod. 13:21)—has become the inner light of faith with which God guides his present-day children on their way through life. Bondage to sin may be experienced despite physical freedom, and freedom in Christ may be experienced despite the social bondage of slavery: "O let us all from bondage flee / And let us all in Christ be free" (17).

Stanza 18 can be understood either as continuing the imagery of the slavery to sin or as referring to the social reality before 1865: "We need not always weep and moan / And wear these slavery chains forlorn." The wording "these slavery chains forlorn" is stiff, stilted, unlike Negro spiritual language; it is more like the forced rhymes in many a well-intended little hymnal of the white overlords, where one could easily find poetry like stanza 19: "This world's a wilderness of woe; / O, let us on to Canaan go."

The last stanzas include typical wandering couplets of
general admonition about the pilgrimage through life and
the temptations of the devil. The figure of the devil plays
no role whatever in the biblical Exodus story. Stanza 22—
"The devil he thought he had me fast, / But I thought I'd
break his chains at last"—takes up the thought of slavery
chains, but now clearly referring, as in many examples
throughout church history, to the enslavement to sin from
which Christ has freed us. This is not to say that a couplet
like this could not be employed as a code. The wandering
couplet in stanza 24, "I'll tell you what I likes de best: / It is
the shouting Methodist," has nothing to do with the prevail-
ing theme or the constant refrain "Let my people go." The
singers simply don't want to quit; they don't want to let
such a powerful song come to an end, and hence add anything
that pops into their minds.

It is most appropriate that it was the *Jubilee* singers who
made this powerful ballad about the deliverance of God's
people famous, because it truly is a "jubilee" song celebrating the "year of jubilee"—the freedom from social as well as
from spiritual slavery. After the children of Israel, the "freed
slaves," settled in the Promised Land of Canaan, the problem
of slavery arose again, this time as a result of brothers getting
deeper and deeper into debt until they were finally forced
to sell their children, their wives, and then themselves into
bond slavery (Neh. 5:1–6). The practice was widespread
throughout the ancient world. However, biblical law modi-
fied and humanized this method of exploitation somewhat
by enforcing different kinds of sabbath-rest for all (Exod.
20:8–10), and by declaring every fiftieth year a "year of jubilee" in which all enslaved Israelites had to be set free (Lev.
25:39–43). Every seven years they had their debts forgiven
and were given a new start in life (Deut. 15:9). Unfortu-
nately, the slave owners of a much later time paid no heed to
these portions of the Bible.

The term *jubilee* in the Christian tradition became widely
used for Christ's paying our debts, paying the ransom, being

our "redeemer"—with his death buying us free from Satan's bondage and granting us the status of free children of God: "For in Christ there is neither free nor slave" (Gal. 3:28). It is appropriate that the *Jubilee* Singers sang jubilantly of being "free at last!"

7.

Joshua Fit de Battle ob Jericho

Joshua fit de battle ob Jericho, Jericho, Jericho;
Joshua fit de battle ob Jericho
An' de walls come tumblin' down.

You may talk about yo' king ob Gideon,
You may talk about yo' man ob Saul;
Dere's none like good ol' Joshua
At de battle ob Jericho.

Up to de walls ob Jericho
He marched with spear in han';
"Go blow dem ram horns," Joshua cried,
"Kase de battle am in my han'.'"

Den de lam' ram sheep horns begin to blow,
Trumpets begin to soun';
Joshua commanded de chillun to shout
An' de walls come tumblin' down.

Dat mornin'
Joshua fit de battle ob Jericho, Jericho, Jericho;
Joshua fit de battle ob Jericho
An' de walls come tumblin' down.

It seems that some men had an argument about who should be declared the favorite hero. Gideon, Saul, and Joshua were the front-runners. Judges 6–8 told of the first candidate, Gideon, the highly successful judge who, after leading a victorious insurrection against the Midianites and freeing his people from exploitation, refused to be crowned king. The spiritual sings of "yo' king ob Gideon" and "yo' man ob Saul," thereby mixing the man Gideon, who was by profession a judge, with Saul, the first king of Israel. The strong and handsome King Saul was the second candidate, but everybody knows that Saul fell deeply into sin and even tried to kill "lit'le David." Therefore, the singer can exult "Dere's none like good ol' Joshua / At de battle ob Jericho."

It was the fall of the walled city of Jericho that enabled Joshua to lead the children of Israel, after their escape from Egyptian slavery, out of the wilderness into the Promised Land. Joshua 6 gives a detailed report of God's command to Joshua, the preparation of the priests and the people, the battle for and destruction of the city, Joshua's curse upon it, and the saving of Rahab and her family because of her having earlier protected the Israelite spies. The singer omits all the details about the occupation of this key city and concentrates only on the deeds of the hero, Joshua, in his most dramatic moment.

The stylized biblical report with its focus on religious processions, does not mention any war activity directly. But the singer reports as if he had fought in the battle himself at Joshua's side. It is not a case of "Joshua said unto the people"; rather Joshua "cried" his commands even as he marched with "spear in han' " towards the wall.

According to the biblical account, "The Lord said unto Joshua, See, I have given into thine hand Jericho." Joshua in turn says to the *people* when the "seven trumpets of rams' horns" are blown by the priests: "Shout; for the Lord hath given *you* the city" (Josh. 6:16). The spiritual does not mention God as the Lord of the battle; instead, hero Joshua is the chief commander who gives the signal for the attack: "Kase de battle am in *my* han'!" To put it pointedly: in the Bible, Joshua is an agent of God for the people; in the spiritual, the people are agents for Joshua.

In order to highlight the intensity of the successful noise, the spiritual mentions "trumpets" separately. It turns the material from which, according to the biblical description, they were made ("trumpets of rams' horns") into a wholly different musical instrument, namely, a horn—not a French horn, but a "lam' ram sheep horn." Animal parents as well as offspring are mentioned—even though a lamb doesn't have horns—in order to express the unique fullness and power of the victorious sound.   That Joshua commands "chillun" rather than troops gives the scene a much more personal, immediate flavor while at the same time emphasizing how God removes barriers for all his people, all his children.

"Dat mornin' " is not warranted by the biblical story. The phrase derives, however, from a suggestion implicit in a previous line, "Trumpets begin to soun'." The specification of the time not only makes perfect sense in the context of the battle for Jericho, but is also a standard line for visions of "dat great gittin' up mornin'," often simply referred to as "dat mornin'," when the dead will rise at the Last Judgment. According to the visions in Revelation, the new day of God's kingdom will dawn with the sound of trumpets. That will be the day when the last walls of separation will fall and all of God's children will enter the "promised land" and be free in their "home at last," where they will "shout for joy." Thus Joshua's battle of Jericho not only delights as a fantastic hero-story out of the past; it also foreshadows ultimate victory for the children of God when the walls of resistance to God's plan will all "come tumblin' down" to the jubilant shouting of all the believers.

This latter interpretation is dominant in a "ring shout" variation—"Joshua fit de battle 'roun' Jericho's wall / An' he kick one brick outer Satan's hall"—in which the singing is accompanied by an acting out of the words in a circular role play. Here the historical event as such is no longer of interest; the concern has turned wholly to the believer's future. The refrain refers clearly to the heavenly "promised land": "I'm–er goin' where dere ain't no mo' dyin'." It summarizes the consoling promise of Revelation 21:4, a passage which has made unbearable living conditions bearable for millions of believers down through the centuries:

> "And God shall wipe away all tears from their eyes; and there shall be no more death, neither sorrow, nor crying, neither shall there be any more pain; for the former things are passed away."

8.

Sometimes I Feel Like a Motherless Chile

1.
Sometimes I feel like a motherless chile,
Sometimes I feel like a motherless chile,
Sometimes I feel like a motherless chile,
Far, far away from home,
A long, long ways from home.

Then I get down on my knees an' pray,
Get down on my knees an' pray.

2.
Sometimes I feel like I'm almost gone,
Sometimes I feel like I'm almost gone,
Sometimes I feel like I'm almost gone,
Far, far away from home,
A long, long ways from home.

Then I get down on my knees an' pray,
Get down on my knees an' pray.

This song was created in a country uniquely made up of people who had all left their "fatherland"—and many had left their "mother tongue" as well. All had gone "a long, long ways from home," though for various reasons. The only natives, the Indians, had been driven from their homeland by the new arrivals, so the feeling of uprootedness was shared by everybody. Most Europeans had come voluntarily, leaving behind a bad situation of physical, religious, or economic hardship in their search for the "promised land" of freedom. Most Africans came involuntarily, entering into a bad situation of hardship and bondage. But life was not easy for any of the early settlers in the new country. The land had to be settled and worked, and farming was different than in their old countries. Everyone had to live without the experience and guidance of forefathers and foremothers.

In African patriarchical society the father provides food, protection, and direction. When there is no father, survival is threatened. Therefore, when an African wishes to express utmost sorrow and misery he may even today use the old

35

saying, "My father is dead." This need not mean that one's physical father is actually deceased, but only that the person who provided support in the past is no longer capable of providing it. "Son," too, and "sister" and "brother" are terms expressive more of spiritual and psychological relationship, bonds of love, mutual help, and support, than of physical blood relationships. Africans, therefore, grasped readily the metaphoric language in Jesus' parable of the lost son: "For this my son was dead, and is alive again" (Luke 15:24).

This understanding of family proved to be extremely valuable for the deported African slaves, who were systematically separated from family and clan and even from countrymen having the same "mother tongue." It helped them to find new "brothers" and "sisters" in their new homeland. The "family of God" held reunion in revival and prayer meetings where all who were present understood themselves as children of the universal God and addressed each other as brothers and sisters. Jesus said, "For whosoever shall do the will of God, the same is my brother, and my sister, and mother" (Mark 3:35). In the African as well as the Christian understanding, the brother or sister is identified not by a blood-relationship of family or race but by the faith-relationship and the experience of care, support, and love.

The spirituals are full of "brother" and "sister" designations. The "father" designation is reserved for God; it is not used very often, however, at least in comparison with the hymns and liturgies of the liturgical churches. The spirituals address God more often as "Lord."

The shift from the African idiom, "my father is dead," to the Afro-American expression "I feel like a *mother*less chile" reflects the fact that after the physical father had been sold the mother was the only lasting provider of care, support, and love. Occasionally mothers and children too were auctioned off in different directions. "Sometimes I feel like a motherless chile, / A long, long ways from home" therefore expresses utmost desperation. This is underscored in the second stanza: "Sometimes I feel like I'm almost gone"—the separation and homesickness have become virtually unbearable.

In that final expression of anguish, when even the family of God seems to fail, the spirituals are seen to have an affinity with the blues. Yet, what a vast difference whether the song ends in total loneliness and lostness, as in most modern songbooks, or whether the old undergirding refrain is retained: "Then I get down on my knees an' pray, / Get down on my knees an' pray." Prayer restores life. It reawakens the sense of belonging, of being a "chile o' God."

Earlier Christian hymns contain numerous examples of the believer's homesickness for his heavenly home, the goal to be reached somewhere ahead on the long, hard, narrow road along which the "pilgrim progresses." "A long, long ways from home" could at times refer to home with mother here, or home in heaven; at times it could also refer to the free North or even Africa. In a few sparse lines the spiritual sketches such a vivid picture of a despairing, homesick person that it invites anyone in similar circumstances to identify with it, and to express his or her longings and sorrow through this deeply moving song.

9.

Rock O' My Soul

A	B
Rock o' my soul in de bosom of Abraham,	Rock-er ma soul in de bosom ob Abraham,
Rock o' my soul in de bosom of Abraham,	Rock-er ma soul in de bosom ob Abraham,
Rock o' my soul in de bosom of Abraham,	Rock-er ma soul in de bosom ob Abraham,
Lord, rock o' my soul.	Oh rock-er ma soul.

Books could be written about the life and influence of A. M. Toplady's hymn written in 1776: "Rock of Ages, cleft for me, / Let me hide myself in Thee." It is printed in many denominational hymnbooks and has become a favorite, loved across the various boundaries separating races and classes. The first two lines appear and reappear in speeches, prayers, songs, and even in advertisements. The phrase "Rock of Ages" has become a kind of "prefab" unit that fits well in a multitude of places. It is a "technical term" or symbol for reliable security, for God's lasting protection from the various dangers which threaten our lives. Since so many spirituals refer to the "rock" image, it is interesting to follow the evolution of the different stages this "prefab" unit has gone through on its way from the Bible to the songs of church folks.

Isaac Watts's famous hymn "Our God, our help in ages past, / Our hope for years to come, / Our shelter from the stormy blast, / And our eternal home" contains many of the constituent elements concentrated in this "prefab" unit. But what is so curious about the lines "Rock of Ages, cleft for me, / Let me hide myself in Thee" is the fact that they represent a complete turnabout, a 180-degree reversal of the biblical story which was the source of this image. Observation of the intermediate steps in this process will show how our perception of God has also changed since Old Testament times, legitimately reversing the ancient image.

Mount Sinai is the point of departure. The children of Israel had successfully escaped from Egyptian slavery. But life in the desert, they found, wasn't as pleasant and easy as they had hoped. One spiritual summarizes their disenchantment:

> Children grumbled on the way,
>   Wish I had died in the Egyptland.
> Children they forgot to pray;
>   Wish I had died in the Egyptland.
>
> Now they wept and now they moaned,
>   Wish I had died in the Egyptland.
> Then they turned around and groaned,
>   Wish I had died in the Egyptland.

While their leader, Moses, had his most profound religious experience receiving there atop Mount Sinai the Ten Commandments on tables of stone, the grumbling children of Israel went wild with a pagan festival, dancing around a golden calf. When he descended from the mountain Moses was so furious over their unfaithfulness that he smashed the tables of stone to pieces (Exod. 31:18–32:19). The people had proven themselves totally unworthy of God's covenant with them.

Moses commanded a drastic purification. He took the golden calf, "burnt it in the fire, and ground it to powder, and strewed it upon the water, and made the children of Israel drink of it" (Exod. 32:20). Then he ordered all the men who had not chosen the Lord's side to be slain with the sword, "and there fell of the people that day about three thousand men" (Exod. 32:28). The next morning Moses returned to the Lord and offered himself as an atonement for the sins of his people (Exod. 32:31–32). But the Lord answered, "Whosoever hath sinned against me, him will I blot out of my book" (Exod. 32:33). This divine threat occurs in the spirituals as a warning to unremorseful sinners

about the final judgment. The deadly seriousness of Moses'
situation before God, however, has been lost in the song
which sees it more like that of an apprentice called by his
boss to do a better job:

> Moses! Moses! come and see,
> I'll tell you what you do for me:
> I want you to let them idols alone,
> Place my law on the tables of stone,
> And you'll be a witness for the Lord. . . .

The biblical Moses was unable to reverse God's firm decision
to appear no longer among his people. However, God promised Moses: "My presence shall go with thee, and I will give
thee rest" (Exod. 33:14). This promise too has been understood as referring to the believer's pilgrimage through life
to a heavenly rest. But Moses was not satisfied with the ver-
bal renewal of God's covenant; he wanted visual assurance
and asked for one more favor: "I beseech thee, show me thy
glory" (Exod. 33:18). Patiently the Lord explained, "Thou
canst not see my face: for there shall no man see me, and live.
And the Lord said, Behold, there is a place by me, and thou
shalt stand upon a rock: And it shall come to pass, while my
glory passeth by, that I will *put thee in a cleft of the rock*,
and will cover thee with my hand while I pass by: And I will
take away mine hand, and thou shalt see my back parts: but
my face shall not be seen" (Exod. 33:20–23). Only after this
experience were the Ten Commandments, the basic constitution for the covenant people, reissued on new tables of stone.

In this highly dramatic passage it is quite clear that Moses
did not hide *in* God, but *from* God. Moses did not have a
bad conscience like the "kings of the earth and the great
men" in John's apocalyptic vision at the end of time (Rev.
6:15), which in many hymns and spirituals has been merged
with this Exodus text. Sinners have good reason to plead
with "the mountains and rocks, Fall on us, and hide us from
the face of him that sitteth on the throne, and from the
wrath of the Lamb" (Rev. 6:16). The Lord himself provided
protection for Moses; "fer Moses was a man of God," asserts

another spiritual. But a mere human being, even one who has served obediently as God's interpreter and spokesman, cannot confront the divine directly "and live." God's strange action was thus life-affirming. He would not allow Moses to approach him directly, because such immediate encounter with the holy God would have destroyed any human. Instead, God hid Moses in a cleft of a rock during this awesome experience, where Moses could grasp, in hindsight, only as much as a human is capable of perceiving.

Deuteronomy reports that Moses, shortly before his death, sang a psalm of praise to the Lord who had led him through such a difficult but significant life: "Ascribe ye greatness unto our God. He is the Rock, his work is perfect" (Deut. 32:3–4). The psalmists repeatedly called God "my rock and my fortress!" One confessed: "He brought me up also out of a horrible pit, out of the miry clay, and set my feet upon a rock, and established my goings, And he hath put a new song in my mouth" (Ps. 40:2–3). Later the prophet Isaiah envisioned a man who would be "as a hiding place from the wind . . . as the shadow of a great rock in a weary land" (Isa. 32:2). The spirituals and hymns contain references to all these various Old Testament images of "rock."

The New Testament was written to proclaim to the people that Jesus is indeed the expected Messiah, or, to use the Greek word, the Christ; he is the fulfillment of what was foreshadowed in the historical events and prophecies of the Old Testament. Thus the apostle Paul could refer to an incident during the long march of the Israelites through the wilderness when they had run out of food and drink, and Moses, finally following God's command, discovered a spring of clear water in a rock. Paul was writing to new Christians who had left their former religious traditions behind and who were now quarreling among themselves about Communion. Paul interpreted the Old Testament story typologically: they "did all drink the same spiritual drink; for they drank of that spiritual Rock that followed them: and that Rock was Christ" (1 Cor. 10:4). During the course of

church history, however, another use of the rock image
gained prominence, one derived from Jesus' saying, "Thou
art Peter, and upon this rock I will build my church, and
the gates of hell shall not prevail against it" (Matt. 16:18).

We seem to be a long way from the "prefab" unit of which
we spoke, the "Rock of Ages," and yet we are right in the
midst of the various confessions to God which throughout
the ages have employed the rock image melted and mixed
in various ways in Christian hymns, spirituals, and revival
songs. The biblical quotations show how man's perception
of God has gradually changed, not only within the Bible but
ever since. The overwhelming terror once associated with
epiphanies of the Almighty himself, involving forces so strong
that Moses had to be protected from the divine power they
conveyed, has gradually shifted over the years to a terror of
the devil, of other human beings, or of apocalyptic natural
catastrophies, from which believers seek and find consolation
in the protection of a loving God. The faithful flee to God
for refuge, as a child frightened by thunder and lightning
cuddles up in his mother's arms. God has been revealed as
merciful, as the only one who throughout the ages gives
ultimate security to all his children in their most awesome
and horrifying experiences. Therefore the reversal of the
Moses image is legitimate: the sinner with a bad conscience
will try to hide in a rock *from* God; the believer, however,
will hide *in* God, his firm rock and shelter. The sinner will
"run to the rocks to hide my face, / and rocks cry out no
hiding place, / there's no hiding place down there," while
the believer will confidently sing "rocks, don't fall on me"
for he has his hiding place in God.

The singer uses an even more intimate picture in calmly
expressing the wish "When the world's on fire I want
Christ's bosom for to be my pillar [pillow]." The tender
image is drawn from the scene of the Last Supper as depicted
in the Gospel of John, where the "beloved disciple" is the
one who "rests on Jesus' bosom." The image radiates a feeling of ultimate consolation and security.

However, a place in the eternal home has to be secured now. One spiritual quotes the wandering couplet "Gawd give Noah de rainbow sign, / He tol' him no mo' watuh but fiah nex' time" in order to impress upon the listeners the apocalyptic urgency: "O get a home in de rock!" An earlier stanza is made up of the two lines of the famous Toplady hymn:

> O rock of ages clef' fo' me, clef' fo' me,
> O rock of ages clef' fo' me,
> O rock of ages clef' fo' me,
> A let-a me hide-a myself in thee.
> I got a home in de rock, don't yuh see, don't yuh see.

The image of "a home in de rock," recalls a parable Jesus once told about a wise man who built his house upon a rock (Matt. 7:24–27). Several spirituals refer to this famous parable, usually contrasting the rock, dependable faith, with sand, aimless insecurity:

> I build my house upon de rock, O yes, Lord!
> No wind, no storm can blow 'em down, O yes, Lord!
>
> I am not like de foolish man, O yes, Lord!
> He build his house upon de sand, O yes, Lord!

Faith in the "Rock of Ages" has built a home for the believer "in-a dat Rock." The biblical comparison "whosoever heareth these sayings of mine, and doeth them, I will *liken* him unto a wise man" has been understood as a concrete faith-reality. Therefore the singer can enumerate other "wise men," other heroes of faith like Paul and like "poor man Lazarus, poor as I" who also have their homes "in-a dat Rock." It follows logically that the rich man from the parable of Dives and Lazarus (Luke 16:19–31) serves as an example of a sinner who has no home "in-a dat Rock," but "when he died he found his home in hell." The singer himself confesses assuredly,

> W'en I die I'm goin' to res',
> I'm goin'-a lay my head on my Jesus breas';
> I got a home in de rock, don't yuh see.

These intimate notions of the beautiful homelife of each believer with God in heaven are literally ages apart from the concept of the Holy of Holies whose direct presence would consume the ordinary human. They picture God not so much as the awesome Righteous Judge, but more as the affectionate and consoling parent, the "Father" whom Jesus asked us to address as *Abba*—which in Jesus' native language was a child's equivalent of "Daddy." Such a loving and concerned God takes upon himself the burdens of the faithful. He takes care of all human worries caused by geographical isolation, sickness, separation from loved ones, death, and even the terrifying catastrophes prophesied for the end of time. Fear has no room in the shelter of this love. The believer can legitimately address this God, who is the foundation of his firm conviction, as "Rock o' my soul."

It is only consistent that another spiritual quotes from Psalm 40:2—"He brought me up also out of a horrible pit, out of the miry clay, and set my feet upon a rock"—but identifies the "rock" with the well-known term: "He pluck-a my feet out de miry clay: he sot dem-a on de firm Rock o' Ages."

Besides the changes in image of the noun "rock" an interesting change from noun to verb can also be observed in the spirituals when the Moses confession "He is a rock in a weary land, a shelter in a time of storm" was incorporated into a Christmas cradlesong:

> Sister Mary had-a but one child,
> Born in Bethlehem,
> And-a every time-a the-a baby cried
> She'd-a rocked him in the weary land.
> She'd-a rocked him in the weary land.

An image from desert country, from "weary land" where a rock was a shelter which enabled people to survive a horrible sandstorm, has here been transformed into a home scene. The noun "rock" has become the verb "to rock," and the scene is now truly human and humane. Christian artists and poets have rarely, if ever, portrayed the Christchild as a cry-

ing baby in a weary situation. Even under the most difficult
of circumstances they have always given mother and child a
serene, heavenly expression. Not so the spirituals. They
never treat Mary with special deference, as humanly or even
religiously superior. Rather, she is a "sister." The believers
can ask: "O Mary, what you goin' to name that pretty little
baby?" They can also learn from her how she stills "every
time" the unhappiness of her crying baby: "She'd-a rocked
him in the weary land." Motherly love is the most assuring
shelter in time of human misery. The mother's rhythmical
rocking of her baby dispels the threatening weariness.

In a less polished Christmas cradlesong, another important
step in the development of the rock imagery can be observed:

> Mary had de leetle baby
> Born in Bethlehem.
> Eb'ry time de baby cry
> She rock in a weary lan'.
> Ain't dat a rockin' all night,
> Ain't dat a rockin' all night,
> Ain't dat a rockin' all night,
> All night long!

In a premedical society, where there were no aspirins or
sedatives around, rocking a sick child all night long was often
the only remedy loving parents could offer. For the sick
children themselves, the closeness and comfort of the parent
meant so much that the singers could visualize themselves, if
not like the poor man Lazarus of Jesus' parable, whose soul
was carried by angels into Abraham's bosom (Luke 16:22),
then like a baby being rocked to sleep:

> Rock-er ma soul in de bosom ob Abraham,
> Oh rock-er ma soul.

The confession of God as the foundation of the believer's
firm conviction, "Lord, rock o' my soul," has thus been transformed into the request, "rock my soul," or, for rhythm's
sake, "rock-er ma soul." The possessive ("of my soul") related to the noun "rock" has now become the object ("my
soul") of the verb "rock."

This "rockin'," however, has received an adult dimension. The rhythmical swaying of the body in singing these songs "all night long" has led for many to cathartic religious ecstasy. The revival camp meetings where hundreds and thousands were "reelin' an' rockin'" all night long are the religious forerunners of today's big commercially promoted rock festivals, where the electronically—and sometimes chemically—induced "highs" and ecstasies usually lack the Christian religious dimension.

10.

It's Me, O Lord

It's me, it's me, it's me, O Lord,
Standing in the need of pray'r;
It's me, it's me, it's me, O Lord,
Standing in the need of pray'r.

1.
Not my brother, not my sister, but it's me, O Lord,
Standing in the need of pray'r;
Not my brother, not my sister, but it's me, O Lord,
Standing in the need of pray'r.

2.
Not my father, not my mother, . . .

3.
Not the preacher, not the deacon, . . .

Perhaps the most Protestant and American of all spirituals is "It's me, O Lord." Unabashedly, almost obnoxiously, the singer insists before the Almighty: "It's me, it's me, O Lord . . . not my brother, not my sister . . . not my father, not my mother . . . not the preacher, not the deacon . . . but it's me, O Lord." The song can be expanded easily by adding other categories of persons who determine our lives, who all too often try to represent God to us and us to God, who offer—sometimes with the best of intentions—some form of mediation. The singer pushes all the would-be mediators aside, because he wants to be heard immediately, directly, personally, in his own right. To be sure, the "need" is for "prayer," but none of the mediators is asked to pray for the singer; his request is for God's help, God's answer to his own personal petition. The stance is humble, but the humble sinner stands upright, at the center, in faith claiming God's direct attention through prayer.

The song expresses the persistent audacity of a human being who, in his or her need, successfully approaches the highest authority, directly following examples commended by Jesus. Right after the teaching of the Lord's Prayer, Luke records the story of the man who bothers his friend with a request at night; the incident culminates in the encouraging assurance: "How much more shall your heavenly Father give the Holy Spirit to them that ask him?" (Luke 11:13). Matthew records the story of the woman who pushes her way through the crowd until she can at least "touch the hem of his garment" to get healed (Matt. 9:20–22), as other spirituals joyously recall. Such faith knows that it will be heard, recognized, and helped. It empowers the individual "to walk this lonesome valley" and "stand his trials all by himself," as another spiritual says concerning the believer and his great example, Jesus. In his lonesomeness and in his trials, even in the "valley of the shadow of death" the believer need "fear no evil: for thou art with me" (Ps. 23:4).

The New Testament affirmed and universalized a tendency which has its origins already in the Old Testament faith— that *all* peoples are God's and that *all* are equal before the Lord. All may become "children of the living God," as Paul put it (Rom. 9:26). Yet the constant human temptation is for some to claim, in Orwell's terms, that they are "more equal than others," so that hierarchies of intermediaries develop again and again.

Martin Luther's sixteenth-century rediscovery of the biblical concept of the priesthood of all believers meant that everybody could pray to God directly, without the intercession of priests, saints, or anyone else. However, this key concept of the Reformer was soon imperiled in the lands of the Reformation by rising new political hierarchies. Many believers fled their homelands and emigrated to America because they refused to let either political or ecclesiastical sovereigns determine their faith. Their protest echoed the affirmation: "Not the . . . but it's me, O Lord."

The new country consciously did away with all the clerical and noble titles that had established ranks of superiority and inferiority in Europe. The only titled offices in most early American churches were preacher, deacon, and elder. But even those offices were experienced by the singer as hindering his direct access to God: "It's not the preacher, not the deacon, but it's me, O Lord." A basic Reformation change in the perception of God and man had been institutionalized among those who despised all forms of dictatorship.

An all-powerful potentate in a strongly patriarchical society generally inspires fear and awe. His underlings, accordingly, seek mediation, good connections, through which they can influence the boss or father; frequently the mother is regarded as the most diplomatic and effective intermediary. Many Africans came from this kind of a family structure, where a son or a servant would prostrate himself before the all-powerful father. It was a form of social organization reflected in many biblical accounts and even in the liturgical customs of some churches. The people who fled such politically enforced structures in Europe and the people who had been deported from Africa into slavery both left that kind of a social order behind. Arrangements and customs that had regulated their lives, for better and worse, were no longer supportive in the new world. In the new land people had to depend spiritually on their own individuality as never before. The slaves, however, had to submit to a much harsher kind of physical dependency under their new masters.

Those who accepted the "local deity" in the new homeland, who asked in their conversion to become children of the Christian God, experienced not the awesome, distant patriarch, but the close, loving, concerned, humane God. The spirituals reflect this "democratic" God, a Lord accessible to all by prayer, regardless of social rank and without mediation of medicine man, priest, ritual, or sacrifice. Not only religious functionaries, but even family members are enumerated in this song as potential hindrances to direct spiritual experience.

Psychologically, it is interesting that the "master" is not mentioned in the first place as the main hindrance to be circumvented. No doubt the master and the mistress were included in some of the more extended versions, but they never became a central part of the spiritual. Such masters could "kill the body, but are not able to kill the soul" (Matt. 10:28), and so could be excluded from those who exercised spiritual power and influence over the slaves even before emancipation. What is even more amazing is the fact that enslaved people could develop such a self-confidence as to say before God, "It's me, it's me!" However, the history of faith and martyrdom reveals many outstanding examples of this confidence in God, which gives believers the courage to stand as boldly as Moses stood before Pharaoh, or Daniel before Nebuchadnezzar. Ever since Jesus prayed for those who executed him it has been possible for Christians to stand firmly and forgivingly, as Paul stood before his jailors and judges, or Martin Luther when he faced kings and cardinals and declared "Here I stand," or Martin Luther King when he stood up to racist mobs and claimed God-given rights. "It's me, O Lord" is a song that resounds with trust in the power of prayer.

11.

Dry Bones

God called Ezekiel by his word,
"Go down and prophesy!"
"Yes, Lord!"
Ezekiel prophesied by the power of God,
Commanded de bones to rise.

Dey gonna walk aroun', dry bones,
Dey gonna walk aroun', wid de dry bones
Dey gonna walk aroun', dry bones,
Why don't you rise an' hear de word of de Lord.
"Tell me, how did de bones get together wid de long bones?
Prophesy?"

Ah, well, de toe bone connected wid de foot bone,
De foot bone connected wid de ankle bone,
De ankle bone connected wid de leg bone,
De leg bone connected wid de knee bone,
De knee bone connected wid de thigh bone,
Rise an' hear de word of de Lord!

Youngsters have lots of fun singing about "dem bones":
"Ah, well, de toe bone connected wid de foot bone, / De foot
bone connected wid de ankle bone . . ." Delighted children
touch each bone of their body while climbing up or down
the musical scale, and because it is so much fun they often
extend the song as far as their anatomical knowledge can
reach. What they do not realize, of course, is that this spiritual was not intended as a nursery-rhyme song for the amusement of children, or even to teach anatomy in a playful man-
ner. They cannot begin to fathom the depth of despair in
which the vision of the dry bones coming together was born.

The people of Israel had been overrun by the political and
military superpower of their time, Babylon, and all the
strong and able people had been captured and carried "a

51

long, long ways from home" into Babylonian captivity to be
used as slave labor.   Their homeland, even their temple,
which was believed to be the dwelling place of God, had been
devastated, plundered, smashed to pieces.   There was no end
in sight for their slavery.   Many hung their harps on the
willow trees and wept at the rivers of Babylon (Ps. 137:1–2).
Their will to live and to serve God had shriveled and dried
up.   More and more of the people had died and the rising
pile of dried-out bones stacking up in the valley indicated
the approaching end of the people of God.   Resignation and
despair hovered over the remnant.

In this totally hopeless situation the word of the Lord is
suddenly heard—and demonstrated.   What happened reminds us of the creation story: God *speaks,* and there *is!* The
prophet Ezekiel recounted his vision: "And as I prophesied,
there was a noise, and behold a shaking, and the bones came
together, bone to his bone" (Ezek. 37:7).   But even after "the
sinews and the flesh came up upon them, and the skin cov-
ered them above"—a process which this spiritual does not
describe—"there was no breath in them" (Ezek. 37:8).   As
Adam, formed out of dust, needed God's breath of life in
order to become a living human being, so "the breath came
into them, and they lived, and stood up upon their feet, an
exceeding great army" (Ezek. 37:10).

Ezekiel's vision of the word of the Lord was tremendously
encouraging to the despairing people: "And ye shall know
that I am the Lord, when I have opened your graves, O my
people, and brought you up out of your graves, And shall
put my spirit in you, and ye shall live, and I shall place you
in your own land" (Ezek. 37:13–14).   The promise culmi-
nated in the restitution of Israel as a people in their own
land.   The word of the Lord transformed their despair into
hope, and the survivors eventually returned home and rebuilt Jerusalem and the temple.

As the Christian tradition repeatedly transferred the expectation of the "promised land" from the geopolitical to

the spiritual level, reinterpreting Israel's pilgrimage from
Egyptian slavery through the desert into Canaan as the proto-
type for each individual on his or her pilgrimage through
the various hardships of life on earth to the glorious heavenly
land, so the expectation of a new rebuilt Jerusalem following
the return from captivity was transferred to a heavenly new
Jerusalem in which the individual would live after death.
Ezekiel's vision of the dry bones became in this figurative
interpretation the prime illustration for the "resurrection of
the body," confidently expected for the end of time at Christ's
return for judgment and final salvation.

"Dem bones" are "my father's," "my mother's," "my
brother's," "my sister's," and "mine."   All will rise again in
that "great gittin' up mornin'," as other spirituals assure,
when the Lord "opens your graves, O my people" (Ezek.
37:13) and gathers all his people together to take them to the
heavenly homeland.   The Lord's "people" are now no longer
only the physical descendants of Abraham, but the believers
of all races, or, as another spiritual about Ezekiel's vision says,
all the "sanctified":

> The wind did blow, the bones did rise.
>   Don't God's children have a hard time?
> None can't enter but the sanctified.
>   Don't God's children have a hard time?

In Ezekiel's vision the bones heard the word of the Lord
and rose.   The spiritual encourages—indeed commands—
discouraged fellow travelers who are ready to slump down at
the wayside to "rise an' hear de word of de Lord!"—Get up,
you lazy bones, hear and accept the word of the Lord!   Become a member of the family of God and you will survive
the hard times here on earth.   Your tired bones will rise and
happily "dey gonna walk aroun'."

The believers' vision of a fulfilled life after death enabled
them to endure the hardships of slavery, sickness, and death,
as it had the captives in ancient Babylon and many other
desperate and deported people throughout history.   It made

them so happy that they could even chuckle in amusement
and shout for joy, imagining how their old bones would be
coming together again, bone by bone. Already they felt the
Spirit moving in their hearts, starting the new creation of
meaningful life even in the situation of pervasive meaning-
lessness.

12.

Go Tell It on the Mountain

Go tell it on the mountain,
Over the hills and ev'rywhere;
Go tell it on the mountain
That Jesus Christ is-a-born.

1.
When I was a sinner,
I prayed both night and day;
I asked the Lord to help me,
And he showed me the way.

2.
When I was a seeker,
I sought both night and day;
I asked my Lord to help me,
And he taught me to pray.

3.
He made me a watchman
upon the city wall;
And if I am a Christian,
I am the least of all.

"Go, tell it . . . ev'rywhere . . . / That Jesus Christ is-a-born."
This imperative has been almost fulfilled: the chorus can
now be heard all over the world, especially during the Christmas season.   Apparently the chorus was the best part of this
Christmas spiritual.   It deeply impressed itself on the memory of all who heard and sang it, and they carried it with
them and shared it wherever they went.   The effect was like
that of a chain letter, though this chain-song was not the
song of a chain gang, but a jubilant song proclaiming the
birth of one who is the liberator from all kinds of bondage—
and this happy news was to multiply exponentially.

The "original" stanza may have spelled out the Christmas
story, but if it existed at all it has been lost.   The chorus was
obviously better formulated and so was handed on even
though the singers just couldn't keep the stanzas in mind—
although they could still hum the tune.   So the singers replaced the stanzas with some of the standards, any favorite
couplets that fitted the tune.   These couplets had been
polished so well by being sung over and over again in other

songs that they were by now smoothly formulated and could easily be learned by heart. For instance:

> When I was a seeker, I sought both night and day,
> I asked the Lord to help me, and he showed me the way.

This wandering couplet, which tells of a conversion experience, is suggested by the Sermon on the Mount: "Seek and ye shall find" (Matt. 7:7). It can be sung in any season and has nothing specifically to do with Christmas.

Nor does the other wandering couplet, which is usually sung as the second stanza:

> He made me a watchman upon the city wall,
> And if I am a Christian, I am the least of all.

It is curious to find in the United States this image of the "city wall." European cities—and those of the biblical lands —were protected with a wall all around, complete with gates, watchtowers, and watchmen on patrol during the night. The famous German hymn "Wachet auf," for example, combines this imagery with the well-known parable of the ten virgins, about which many spirituals also sing:

> Wake, awake, for night is flying;
> The watchmen on the heights are crying,
> Awake, Jerusalem, at last!
> The Bridegroom comes, awake;
> Your lamps with gladness take;
> Alleluia!
> And for his marriage feast prepare,
> For ye must go to meet him there.

The prophet Isaiah painted for his countrymen in Babylonian captivity a glorious vision of the restored earthly Jerusalem. His image was understood centuries later as a reference to the heavenly "new Jerusalem" with its golden streets and pearly gates, as the Book of Revelation paints it in even more glorious colors. "I have set watchmen upon thy walls, O Jerusalem" (Isa. 62:6) was understood to refer to the one who would announce the coming of the Lord, as in the parable of the ten virgins: "At midnight there was a cry made, Behold, the bridegroom cometh; go ye out to meet him" (Matt. 25:6). The singer now considers himself the watchman, who will have the honor of seeing the Lord come and of announcing this most important news to all fellow believers.

Other parables of the heavenly marriage feast describe how "the least" on the social ladder are invited to enjoy the celebration. In Matthew's vision of the Last Judgment the king holds everybody accountable for their actions during their earthly life. He decides who will inherit the kingdom. The righteous, unaware of their good deeds, ask him:

> Lord, when saw we thee ahungered, and fed thee? or thirsty, and gave thee drink? When saw we thee a stranger, and took thee in? or naked, and clothed thee? Or when saw we thee sick, or in prison, and came unto thee? And the King shall answer and say unto them, Verily I say unto you, Inasmuch as ye have done it unto one of *the least* of these my brethren, ye have done it unto me.   (Matt. 25:37–40)

The second line of the couplet "And if I am a Christian, / I am the least of all" is ambiguous. Does "the least" imply that the singer was in the greatest need for help? Or does it refer to the humility which Paul could express when he said, "I am the least of the apostles" (I Cor. 15:9)? Or could it indicate the faithfulness of believers: "He that is faithful in that which is least is faithful also in much" (Luke 16:10)?

Because several stanzas have nothing specifically to do with Christmas, the chorus is occasionally changed in its very last words:

> Go tell it on the mountain,
> Over the hills and everywhere;
> Go tell it on the mountain
> That Jesus Christ is-a-Lord.

His Lordship can be proclaimed at all times, not just at Christmas, and should be proclaimed everywhere as the parting Lord commanded his disciples: "Go ye therefore and teach all nations . . ." (Matt. 28:19).

Instead of adjusting the text of the chorus to the new

stanzas, some people have gone in the opposite direction and created new stanzas more suitable to the old Christmas chorus. Some of these stanzas are contained in more recent church hymnals:

1.
While shepherds kept their watching
O'er silent flocks by night,
Behold throughout the heavens
There shone a holy light.

2.
The shepherds feared and trembled
When lo! above the earth
Rang out the angel chorus
That hailed our Savior's birth.

3.
Down in a lowly manger
The humble Christ was born,
And God sent us salvation
That blessed Christmas morn.

This poetry is a good example of hymnal language, but a bad example of folk-song language. It utilizes the grammar and vocabulary people use when they sit next to each other in church pews and sing to the accompaniment of soft organ music words they read from a book. This is not the language they would use "on the mountain, over the hills and everywhere" in telling a story to each other. The trouble with these secondary stanzas is that they are still too much of an "original."

There are no "originals" in folklore, no tunes or texts that are the copyrighted possession of a talented individual and may be reproduced for a fee but never criticized and altered to fit other people's needs. We can be glad that the first stanzas of the spirituals are in fact lost, for "originals" in folklore are like a big coarse piece of rock that falls into a river. Only after it has been carried along in the stream for years and years, in all kinds of weather, tumbling against other rocks in fast rushing torrents and lying quietly in almost still waters as the gentle currents slide endlessly by, only after it had stood the test of time and lost its rough edges and nonessential additions, only then is it smooth and beautiful enough to fit every hand, and so beautiful that everybody likes to touch it, feel it, and show it to his friends. Only then can everybody easily and gladly hand it on from sister to brother, from generation to generation.

The refining process of oral tradition has polished the Christmas chorus of this particular spiritual until it has become a shining "diamond." But the "original" stanzas obviously did not pass the test: those first texts were forgotten. And those modern "original" stanzas desperately need the rock-tumbling process; they do not yet rest and nest in a person's mind because they are not yet the folk's language, not yet folk songs of the common people. Educated church people obediently sing what they see printed in their hymnal, but the lyrics do not follow them home; they are not yet in a form which easily engraves itself upon the heart and then "comes from the heart," as do so many of the gems that have been purified in the long process of oral tradition.

This song experienced drastic adaptation in the 1960s, in two different directions, when it was employed in concrete political situations in Mississippi and in Birmingham, Alabama. Had they not appeared in print, these dated *ad hoc* versions would already have been forgotten, like countless other variations and versions of spirituals and folk songs before printing and recording was so easy.

The Mississippi version incorporated the refrain of the famous spiritual "Go Down, Moses," with its reference to Exodus 5:1: "Thus saith the Lord God of Israel, Let my people go." The chorus of the old Christmas spiritual then read:

> Go tell it on the mountain,
> Over the hills and everywhere;
> Go tell it on the mountain
> To let my people go!

The Birmingham version substituted a different last line: "That freedom is coming soon." It also adapted the old wandering couplet:

> I would not be a sinner;
> I'll tell you the reason why:
> I'd be afraid my Lord might call me
> And I would not be ready to die.

It also replaced the word "sinner" with the names of specific political figures who were opposing the then current struggle for freedom, some of whom actually heard the message, decided to change their position, and since have aided the coming of freedom for all.

Histories such as these indicate the vitality of folk songs: they can be adapted again and again to serve various congregations in specific times of need. Yet they have a polished essence which transcends the times, a core message which lives on in song—even where there is no crisis—and is enjoyed throughout the world, a universally valid proclamation of the good news that "Jesus Christ is-a-born" and that he brings transforming love with him wherever he is accepted.

13.

Let Us Break Bread Together

1.
Let us break bread together on our knees;
Let us break bread together on our knees.
When I fall on my knees, with my face to the rising sun,
O Lord, have mercy on me.

2.
Let us drink wine together on our knees . . .

3.
Let us praise God together on our knees . . .

This spiritual, which in its older versions started with "Let us praise God together on our knees," is unusual in two respects: It invites to Communion, a central Christian custom which finds hardly any mention in the other spirituals, and its refrain, "When I fall on my knees, with my face to the rising sun . . .," is of uncertain interpretation.

Some see the kneeling towards the east as a reference to an Islamic custom. According to the Koran the Muslim is required to pray at certain hours of the day, falling down on his knees and touching his prayer rug with his forehead facing Mecca, the holy city of Islam, which—for Mohammed's people—lay to the east. But these prayers are offered also when the sun is in the west. Moreover, Jerusalem as well as Mecca lies in the east. Jews at prayer orient themselves toward Jerusalem. It seems improbable that a memory of Islamic worship, or sun-worship, has influenced this quiet reverent spiritual, as some claim.

The song is definitely Christian in its reference to the sharing of bread and wine in Communion. Communion

was sometimes celebrated at Easter sunrise services, and early
morning worship has always held a special attraction for
Christians. Wine of course is absolutely prohibited in the
Islamic religion. This song of togetherness in God's Communion has found acceptance in almost all the established
Christian churches, even those where kneeling is not prac-
ticed, either for receiving the elements or for public or pri-
vate prayer.

There is also an old Christian burial tradition which required that the corpse be buried with the head toward the
east. Believers wanted to be facing the rising sun, since they
expected that Christ—who rose on Easter *morning*—would
return "in that great gittin' up *mornin'* " and call the believers out of their graves first.

The last line of every stanza, "O Lord, have mercy on me,"
has an intriguing dimension far beyond the familiar liturgical
use. "Lord, have mercy on me"—in Greek *Kyrie eleison*—
was the pleading cry an important person in the ancient
world would hear when needy people along the roadside fell
down on their knees to beseech him. If he felt like it he
would grant their request; if not he might order them
whipped and dragged out of his way. The Gospels tell of
several needy people who approached Jesus with this cry,
pleading for healing though, not for money. Matthew mentions two unnamed blind men (Matt. 20:30–34); Mark tells
of Bartimaeus (Mark 10:46–52). All cried for help when
they heard that this Jesus was passing by. His disciples didn't
want to be bothered with these beggars and tried to shut
them up, but Jesus took personal care of the "unimportant";
he "gave de blind his sight"—as other spirituals rejoice—and
transformed miserable social outcasts of society into jubilant
followers.

The story about the Canaanite woman (Matt. 15:21–28)
was even more offensive to the ruling classes of Jesus' time—
and even more consoling and encouraging to the singers.
She was, moreover, a foreigner, and not at all of the pres-

tigious kind—any "decent" rabbi would have had nothing to do with a Canaanite, much less talk theology with a woman. The disciples acted according to custom when they sought to "send her away." Jesus at first "answered her not a word," and then finally rebuked her: he was sent only to the "lost sheep of Israel" and "it is not meet to take the children's bread, and to cast it to dogs." But this woman was as persistent as Jacob wrestling with the angel (Gen. 32:24–29)— with whom the spiritual singers could readily identify: "I had a mighty battle like-a Jacob an' de angel"; "When yo' bless muh soul, I'll let yo' go"; "I didn't 'tend to lef' 'em go / Till Jesus bless my soul." She fought for the life of her daughter and, falling down on her knees before him, countered Jesus' argument: "Yet the dogs eat of the crumbs which fall from their master's table." Jesus marveled: "O woman, great is thy faith," and he healed her daughter. The Canaanite woman's persistent faith became an encouraging example throughout the centuries, especially when well-to-do believers were unwilling to share God's love with the sociably less acceptable.

The situation of the slaves, who were treated like dogs living off the crumbs from their master's table, had many similarities to that of the Canaanite woman. It is reported that some "disciples" of Jesus wanted them turned out of the churches because they wept too loudly when certain biblical stories were read. Other "disciples" were not sure whether one should allow slaves to become Christians at all, because one could not easily hold a *brother* or *sister* in Christ as a *slave*. Others went even further and forbade all Bible reading for slaves; they even set a punishment on anyone who would teach slaves how to read for themselves—lest they read not only liberating passages from the Bible but also abolitionist literature. Again, others argued that making the slaves Christians would make them better slaves—"Servants, obey in all things your masters . . . fearing God" (Col. 3:22)—and they portrayed God as a super-overseer.

The singers continued to cry, "O Lord, have mercy on me." And their persistent cry penetrated the walls of convenience and custom men had erected—until God finally gave the blind their sight and made it possible for all of us, descendents of slaves as well as of masters, to "break bread together on our knees."

14.

Hold On!

Keep your hand on-a dat plow!
   Hold on!
Hold on! Hold on!
Keep your hand right on-a dat plow!
   Hold on!

1.
Noah, Noah, lemme come in,
Doors all fastened an de winders pinned.
Keep your hand on-a dat plow!
Noah said, You done lost yo' track,
Can't plow straight an' keep a-lookin' back.

2.
Sister Mary had a gold chain;
Every link was my Jesus' name.
Keep your hand on-a dat plow!
Keep on plowin' an' don't you tire;
Every row goes hi'er an' hi'er.

3.
Ef you wanner git to Heben
I'll tell you how:
Keep your hand right on-a dat plow!
Ef dat plow stays in-a your hand,
Land you straight in de Promise' Land

We have observed how some songs gradually received their proper shape in the "rock-tumbling process" of oral tradition. Another interesting aspect of the process is the disintegration of songs into discrete units and the creation of new songs out of various isolated units. The result can be like a mosaic made up of different well-polished stones, as may be clearly seen in "Hold On!"

The most recent step in this process produced a song made popular by Pete Seeger, which was usually sung as, "Hold on! Hold on! Keep your eyes on the prize! Hold on!"—though sometimes "prize" was replaced with "price." This simple refrain, which has been so instrumental in exhorting people to pull together and strive for a common goal in the Civil Rights movement, has come a long way from its original setting in a farming society: "Keep your hand on-a dat plow! Hold on!" The plow in turn comes from a well-known saying of Jesus: "No man, having put his hand to the plow, and looking back, is fit for the kingdom of God" (Luke 9:62).

The spiritual sees the "gospel plow" as a concrete faith-reality, not as an abstract metaphor. This faith-reality is not tied to any specific person or historical period. Thus, Jesus' words could be put in Noah's mouth as Noah's explanation of why some lost their way to heaven: "Noah said, You done lost yo' track, / Can't plow straight an' keep a-lookin' back."

Why Noah? Noah is the prime biblical example of straightforward obedience in the face of all temptations to "backslide." The spiritual "Tell me, who built the ark?" recounts: "The wicked did laugh. / They called old Noah the foolish man, / Because Noah built his ark upon dry land." However, Noah's "foolishness," his stubborn determination to obey God's command whatever the odds—and fads—paid off: Noah was safe in the ark when the devastating flood came. The singers' interest was not in Noah, but in encouraging anyone tempted to give up: "Keep your hand on-a dat plow! *Hold on!*"

The first two lines of the first stanza have been taken from another Noah-song which described the situation in greater detail:

> When the ark was finished it began to rain;
> Women and children began to scream,
> Say, O Noah, let me in!
> Noah he cry: The door is fasten, and the winder pin;
> God came down, lock the door,
> Take the key back to heaven with him.

Here the situation at the ark as one of judgment is fused with the slave's life experience and the New Testament admonition for the final judgment:

> Strive to enter in at the strait gate: for many, I say unto you, will seek to enter in, and shall not be able. When once the master of the house is risen up, and hath shut the door, and ye begin to stand without, and to knock at the door, saying, Lord, Lord, open unto us; and he shall answer and say unto you, I know you not whence you are.   (Luke 13:24–25)

The second stanza of the spiritual begins with a totally unrelated couplet: "Sister Mary had a gold chain; / Every link was my Jesus' name." The couplet seems to mix the rosary with symbols from old Scottish folk ballads that had migrated along to the new country. "Gold chain" and "silver spade" were symbols of nobility referred to in ballads about the burial of aristocrats, their lovers from among the commoners, and even their dogs. The grave would be dug with a silver spade and the body lowered into the grave with a golden chain while the mourners called the name of the deceased. The symbols of aristocracy lost their original meaning in the life-reality of America's frontier democracy and became merely images for pretty and precious decorations, which in turn became the common property of folklore.

Whether "Sister Mary" refers to the mother of Jesus in a pietà scene, or to a believer saying a rosary type of prayer and calling Jesus' name with every link or bead, cannot be determined. The "original" context is lost and various singers may have attributed various meanings to these relics from a different context. The earlier singers surely knew what *slave* chains were, and that they were not at all golden.

A beautiful transformation of the image of enforced exploitation was born during the Freedom movement: "The only chain that a man can stand / Is the chain of hand in hand." "Hold on" to your fellowman; strengthen each other in the common struggle of life until you can even sing: "We've met jail and violence too, / But God's love has seen us through. Hold on!"

The couplet concluding the second stanza embellishes the image of the plow by pairing it with a line from "Jacob's Ladder": "Ev'ry round goes higher 'n' higher." A vertical image, the ladder on which the believer hopes to ascend to heaven, is fused with the horizontal image of plowing in rows:

> Keep on plowin' an' don't you tire;
> Every row goes hi'er and hi'er.

The last stanza of the spiritual finally gives the recipe directly:

> Ef you wanner git to Heben
> I'll tell you how:

> Keep your hand right on-a dat plow!
> Ef dat plow stays in-a your hand,
> Land you straight in de Promise' Land.

Here for the first time all stanza lines are connected by rhyme as well as reason.

The modern adaptation of the refrain—from "Keep your hand on-a dat plow! Hold on!" to "Keep your eyes on the prize [or, price]! Hold on!"—reminds us of Paul when he admonished the wavering to keep steadfast in their faith. He used an image from the Olympic games which was more familiar and precious to the city dwellers of Corinth than the image of plowing (I Cor. 9:24). American slaves knew much about plowing, while nobody could afford the luxury of sports. Today the "prize" in competitive sports and the "price" in a money economy demand everybody's attention. Hence the contemporary image oscillates between sports and the economy. For some, the goal is no longer the "prize" which God will award the steadfast believer at the end of his or her earthly course. The "price" is rather what people will have to pay in order to reach the goals of social reform for today as well as tomorrow. The "prize" will be freedom and rights. The concept of eternity, which was such a driving force in the early spirituals and hymns, plays no role in many newer versions. Still, individuals are being asked, as in the old songs, to be wise about the investment of their personal sacrifices and to hold on to a worthwhile cause even in difficult times. Today's refrain is "Right on!"

I cannot agree with those who claim that the theological dimension was totally lost at the height of the Civil Rights movement, because even then a central song proclaimed:

> Before I'd be a slave,
> I'd be buried in my grave
> And go home to my Father and be free.

But I do acknowledge that when the willingness to die in nonviolent fashion for the justice in which one believes is lost, a movement for change becomes violent.

15.

Were You There
When They Crucified My Lord?

1.

Were you there when they crucified my Lord?
Were you there when they crucified my Lord?
Oh! Sometimes it causes me to tremble,
   tremble, tremble.
Were you there when they crucified my Lord?

2.

Were you there when they nailed him
   to the tree? . . .

3.

Were you there when they pierced him
   in the side? . . .

4.

Were you there when the sun refused
   to shine? . . .

5.

Were you there when they laid him
   in the tomb? . . .

(6.)

Were you there when he rose up from
   the dead? . . .

1.

They crucified my Lord
An' he never said a mumbalin' word.
They crucified my Lord
An' he never said a mumbalin' word;
Not a word, not a word, not a word.

2.

They nailed him to the tree
An' he never said a mumbalin' word .

3.

They pierced him in the side
An' he never said a mumbalin' word .

4.

The blood came twinklin' down
An' he never said a mumbalin' word .

5.

He bow'd His head and died,
An' he never said a mumbalin' word .

"Were you there?" What a question!

"No! Naturally not! How could we have been? We live almost 2000 years later!"

But that is an irrelevant answer. For the spirituals, time gaps just don't count. Throughout those two thousand years God's love has been crucified, hanged, murdered, quenched, suffocated, gassed, bombed millions of times over, in everybody's lifetime, and *nobody* can deny having been an eye-witness!

Were you there—each verse asks the question—when they (the righteous opponents of God's dynamic love) crucified (killed cruelly and brutally in front of many spectators) my (the one who is dear to me) Lord (him who is more important to me than any master, boss, or ruler)? Were you there as a silent, or even a cheering, bystander? Or were you there perhaps as a participant?

Just imagine what people can do! What *you* are capable of doing! Isn't it frightening? "Oh! Sometimes it causes me to tremble, tremble, tremble." Believers now, as then, find it hard to understand that people can and do watch other human beings suffer. We stand by and watch them hounded, mocked, ridiculed, abused, maltreated, and terrorized, even unto death. Sometimes we lend a hand in the process. Sometimes we merely look on, unable or unwilling to risk our lives—or lifestyles—to stop the cruelty.

"Were *you* there when they nailed him to the tree?" Each stanza repeats the question, three times, so slowly and with such intensity, that we can hardly avoid seeing ourselves in the scene. We have the feeling of being there, involved, right in the midst of the brutality.

The New Testament usually speaks of the "cross" instead of the "tree" (Acts 5:30; 10:39; 1 Pet. 2:24) but a law in the Old Testament legal code required that a man who had suffered the penalty of capital punishment by being "hung on a tree" should be removed before nightfall, "for he that is hanged is accursed of God" (Deut. 21:22–23). Paul showed how God transformed this curse into a blessing: "Christ hath redeemed us from the curse of the law, being made a curse for us: for it is written, Cursed is everyone that hangeth on a tree" (Gal. 3:13).

In contrast to the late twentieth-century United States, where even the electric chair is being banished, the early singers of this spiritual had all too often watched a man lynched and hung on a tree to die. Although they trembled with wrath and fear, their undergirding faith was that God could transform even this curse into a blessing. Trembling faith was the only possible life-affirming response for the politically powerless slaves and their early descendants.

In contrast to many later hymns, paintings, and crucifixes, the New Testament accounts reflect little of the physical pain Jesus experienced. The churches through which most of the slaves received their faith emphasized the *empty* cross as a symbol for the risen Lord who had overcome all suffering. Indeed the Gospels do not dwell on the pain and suffering at all; they simply state that Jesus was crucified. The only way we know that he was "nailed" to the cross is from the report about Thomas testing "the print of the nails" in the risen Lord's hands (John 20:25–27). The Gospel writers did not ask for empathy with the sufferer or abhorrence of his killers; Luke even reports the sufferer's plea, "Father, forgive them; for they know not what they do" (Luke 23:34). Instead the Gospels invite a response of faith to God's life-creating action in and beyond this horrible death.

The spirituals, however, give greater attention to the acts of torment. They even cite as additional cruelty what John took to be a token of more humane treatment than a normal criminal would receive. The evangelist reports that Pilate granted Jesus' friends the favor of being allowed to take his body down earlier than usual. The soldiers, however, were duty-bound to make sure that any crucified person was dead; they usually broke the bones just to be sure. In the case of Jesus, though, they hesitated to do this; instead they tested his blood. When they pierced his side, and water and blood—which believers understood as symbols of Baptism and Holy Communion—came out, the soldiers knew for sure that Jesus was dead and could now be taken down from the cross/tree. John interprets all these happenings as a fulfillment of Old Testament prophecy: "For these things were done, that the scripture should be fulfilled, A bone of him shall not be broken. And again another scripture saith, They shall look on him whom they pierced" (John 19:36–37). The spirituals enumerate this piercing of Jesus' side as one more act of torture before his death.

An extensive version of this spiritual includes Passion and Easter along with the Crucifixion: "Dey whipped him up Calvary . . . Dey led him to Pilate's bar . . . Dey nail him to de cross . . . Dey pierced him in de side . . . He hung his head and died . . . Dey laid him in de tomb . . . He rose up f'om de dead." The mood of this spiritual is very different, depending on whether it ends with this truly happy ending of the resurrection—which converts the tremble of horror into the tremble of awe and joyful expectation—or simply with the death and burial.

Another version, which culminates in the victory of the ungodly destructive forces, mentions also the sun as a cosmic spectator: "The sun refused to shine," a formulation which recurs in the third stanza of the rather complicated hymn, "Saw ye my Savior":

> Jesus hung bleeding,
> Jesus hung bleeding,
> Three dreadful hours in pain;
> Whilst the sun refused to shine
> When his majesty divine
> Was derided, insulted, and slain.

The spiritual asks directly "Were you there when the sun refused to shine?" Both songs refer back to Matthew's account of a midday cosmic shock at the crucifixion of the Son of God: "There was darkness over all the land" (Matt. 27:45). The songs make the sun a feeling agent, who will not give light to such sinister dealings.

The "white hymn" asks the rhetorical question "Saw ye?" in order to continue teaching doctrine: "Oh! He died on Calvary / To atone for you and me / And to purchase our pardon with blood." The spiritual constantly repeats the question "Were you there?" intensifying it to the point of an unyielding interrogation which will not allow *anyone* to hide behind the unfeeling, uncaring attitude of somebody else: even the sun had courage enough to refuse to cooperate!

What did *you* do when you were there, where God's love was murdered? The disgusted trembling over what others have done becomes the shameful trembling over what we ourselves have failed to do.

The lyrics of this powerful spiritual, which makes us both wince in shame and rise to our responsibility, seem to belong to a repertoire of succinct formulations into which the Gospel accounts of Jesus' passion have been crystallized by the empathetic faith of many believers. The verses are so compact and polished in their formulation of the highlights of this deeply moving story that they could easily be "learned by heart" and "kept in mind" and thus reappear whenever somebody intoned a song on the crucifixion or resurrection having roughly the same rhythmic pattern.

The response "Hammering" appropriately accents some versions of the nailing on the tree. It may have been sung by the chain gangs working on the roads and railroads. "An' he never said a mumbalin' word, not a word, not a word, not a word" is the response in numerous other versions sung to a different tune. Jesus' refusal to defend himself in a court which had no Fifth Amendment has puzzled many a reader and listener. He had been such a powerful speaker, had done such mighty deeds, had given the Pharisees such effective back talk that on many occasions they were actually dumbfounded and speechless. Why did he now refuse to invoke the powers of God in order to save his own skin? He even angered the powers-that-be with his passive resistance to their schemes rather than trying to please them by humbly pleading for his life; before Pilate "he answered him to never a word" (Matt. 27:14). Matthew noted Jesus' silence in order to portray him as the true sacrificial "Lamb of God who takest away the sins of the world," as the Angus Dei puts it in many a Communion liturgy, the one who fulfilled Isaiah's prophecy of the "suffering servant" bringing salvation to Israel: "He was oppressed, and he was afflicted, yet he opened not his mouth: he is brought as a lamb to the slaughter" (Isa. 53:7).

A hymn had formulated it: "He gave his soul up to the stroke, without a murmuring word." The spiritual intensifies the marvel. Jesus not only refused to speak in his own defense; he didn't even mumble a subdued curse: "An' he never said a mumbalin' word." Jesus' silence at his trial so impressed the slaves—who themselves had to be silent in the face of trials and executions—that it was transposed into a major theological statement. The freed children of Israel murmured against God in the wilderness and looked back with longing to slavery in Egypt: "Children grumbled on the way, / 'Wish I had died in the Egyptland'." As a punishment they died in the desert and never entered the Promised Land (Num. 14:2, 26–32). The spirituals on the crucifixion thus imply that Jesus, because he did not murmur against God, is able to lead us all into the eternal "promised land."

Matthew and the other Gospel writers do not portray Jesus as totally silent. Together they transmit a total of "seven words" that he spoke from the cross. At least one version of a crucifixion spiritual, "Look-a how dey done muh Lawd," made a stanza of the "seventh word": "He cried, Eli, eli." But the same song nevertheless also included as one stanza the well-known refrain, "He never spoke a mumbalin' word."

Again, basically identical formulations make up the verses of the various spirituals on the crucifixion and the resurrection. The songs were written down only after they had been well rounded out in the "rock-tumbling process" of oral tradition for a considerable period of time and had become standardized "pre-fab" units out of which new songs could easily and quickly be constructed.

One stanza, which is occasionally added after "They nailed him to the tree" or "They pierced him in the side," took a strange yet interesting journey into other contexts as it tumbled. In it the singer envisions the crucified Lord, with nails driven through his hands and his side slit open, bleeding: "De blood run down." In other versions the line may read: "The blood come streamin' down," or again, more restrained, "The blood come tricklin' down," or even "a-twink-a-lin' down." The sermonlike interpretation, formulated in one version as "He die for you and me," has caused an unfortunate contraction of images, which simply doesn't make much sense any more as formulated in a new lively song: "Love come a-tricklin' down."

Here a sentence which in hymns and spirituals once vividly described a visual occurrence has been interpreted theologically in a different frame of reference, that of religious sacrifice: Jesus' blood was the sufficient sacrifice once and for all offered in *love*. Thus "blood" in the earlier line is replaced by "love" in the later formulation. But now the verb "tricklin' down" conveys the impression of stinginess. God's love is usually said to be "poured out" or "given freely" so that the "cup overflows." The old-time spirituals could marvel again and again that God is *not* a miser, that he gives freely and generously: "Did you ever see such a man as God, / Who gave up his son for to come and die, / Who gave up his son for to come and die, / Just to save my soul from a burning fire?" A new gospel song, however, combines the "trickle down" with a favorite saying from Matthew (7:7):

> Seek and ye shall find,
> Knock and the door shall open,
> Ask and it shall be given,
> And the love come a-tricklin' down.

In this context everything seems light, easy, almost mechanically automatic—far removed from the depth of faith which gave birth to the profoundly moving texts of the spirituals, "They crucified my Lord" and "He never said a mumbalin' word."

The western church, which has witnessed countless tortures and executions of believers, has long emphasized the last *words* of Jesus. The slaves in their spirituals emphasize his *silence*. Why? Those who admire Jesus' pliant acceptance of unjust treatment and even execution without open rebellion have drawn seething criticism from Marx, Nietzsche, and many a modern ideologue. These critics do not grasp that Jesus' attitude was born not of weakness but of divine strength. To curse persecutors is merely to react at their level. But Jesus said: Act! "Bless them that curse you . . . and persecute you" (Matt. 6:44). To bless is the last act of free will in a situation totally dominated by others. Love is the only act which can open the future to good, even for the executioner. At the same time, dying with dignity in the face of certain annihilation is a testimony to a freedom which cannot be enslaved by an earthly master; it defies the power of the enemy and the finality of death. The blood of the martyrs became the seed of the church as long as they were executed in public, as long as their last words and their way of accepting death could make a lasting impression on both executioners and spectators. Indeed, this is why modern dictators are very careful to have resisters tortured and executed in secret. Technical "progress" in the means of mass annihilation, from the rope to the guillotine to the gun to the gas chamber and finally to the nuclear bomb, has made even this last act of individuality ineffective as a witness to others.

The early Americans were no strangers to beatings and hangings. Christian slaves obviously admired Jesus' ability to suffer such punishment and persecution without "mumblin' a word" of complaint. It must have been consoling for the Africans in American slavery to be able to identify with other enslaved humans who had found a point of reference for understanding their plight. Slaves in New Testament times had been able to make unjust cruelty meaningful, and therefore endurable, when they saw it as a "call" to follow Christ's example, to experience unjust suffering as he did—without complaint, as they were admonished in 1 Peter 2:18–25. This call is coupled with the hope that "he that hath suffered in the flesh [like Christ] hath ceased from sin" (1 Pet. 4:1). There are numerous other passages in the New Testament written specifically to console the first martyrs; they speak of believers joining "the fellowship of his sufferings" (Phil. 3:10) in order to be "children of God" and "joint-heirs with Christ," so that they would also be "glorified together" with him in heaven (Rom. 8:16–17). To suffer was a part of what it meant to be "counted worthy of the Kingdom of God" (2 Thess. 1:5), and that was something to sing about. This joy, however, was severely tested where white masters misused biblical texts in order to justify their unchristian behavior, where slave owners ignored the biblical admonitions that they shared the same Master (Col. 4:1), who was not a respecter of persons (Acts 10:34) and who would reward slave and master alike for doing good (Eph. 6:8–9).

At the other extreme, some people in the history of the church have masochistically sought out suffering and coveted martyrdom in order to be counted especially worthy of the kingdom. Jesus was neither a masochist nor a sadist. In raising him from death God demonstrated once and for all that no human cruelty or misery can separate us from his love (Rom. 8:35–39). It is the experience of this love that makes the faithful sing.

16.

Chillun, Did You Hear When Jesus Rose?

Chillun, did you hear when Jesus rose,
Did you hear when Jesus rose;
Chillun, did you hear when Jesus rose,
He rose an' ascended on high!

1.
Mary set her table
In spite of all her foes;
King Jesus sat at de center place
An' cups did overflow.

2.
The Father looked at his Son an' smiled,
De Son did look at-a him;
De Father saved my soul from hell
An' de Son freed me from sin.

When Roland Hayes, the famous soloist, sings "The Life of Christ as Told Through Aframerican Folksong" and asks quietly and inquisitively, "Were you there when they crucified my Lord?" we may at first try to defend ourselves. But soon we realize how hollow our arguments sound. So far from excusing us, they actually accuse us for letting such atrocities happen over and over again. Events that should have moved us to intervene for God's sake have instead made us forsake God and stand aside, aloof, uninvolved, as if we were watching a movie or TV program totally unrelated to reality. This penetrating question "Were you there?" gradually draws us into a state of trepidation and judgment. Our mumbling self-defenses disintegrate until finally not a word, not a word, will come.

Into this silence Hayes suddenly shouts another question: "Chillun, did you hear when Jesus rose?" His song now is fast and joyous. Its rhythm vibrates contagiously through us, raising our spirits, moving us emotionally from dispassionate distance to joyous engagement, saving us from our own personal hell. This outstanding news has to be repeated over and over again: Jesus rose, "He rose an' ascended on high!"

The spiritual completes the rising motion and then describes the risen Son's arrival in heaven in terms of a beautiful family scene with a happy reunion dinner. Unlike medieval portraits in which the mother of the Lord is regally attended by angels and saints, the spiritual portrays Mary as a busy housewife attending herself carefully to her practical family obligations: "Mary set her table." The singers envisioned this heavenly scene in terms of the best they knew here on earth, supported of course by the imagery of the most widely known psalm, that of the "Good Shepherd":

> Thou preparest a table before me
>   in the presence of mine enemies:
> Thou anointest my head with oil;
>   my cup runneth over . . .
> and I will dwell in the house of the Lord
>   for ever.   (Ps. 23:5–6)

In the spiritual Mary tends to her motherly duties "in the house of the Lord"; she sets her table "in spite of all her foes." What foes? The "enemies" of the psalmist have become Mary's "foes," but the spiritual does not say who they are. Son Jesus has earned the honorary title "King," and therefore deserves the "center place" at the table. The presence of a king transforms the intimate family dinner into a banquet of royal abundance: "An' cups did overflow." The feast of plenty celebrated in heaven on high is one which every believer would like to attend.

While the mother cares for the food, the father looks proudly at his son and smiles, thoroughly pleased with what his son has accomplished. The scene reminds us of a famous song-sermon on the Creation where God's smile causes the creation of light and God concludes "That's good!" (cf. Gen. 1:3–9). The deep-seated satisfaction that accompanied the first creation is expressed here with respect to the second creation, the work of redemption. The singers see the job as divided between Father and Son: "De Father saved my soul from hell / An' de Son freed me from sin." The interplay of the designations "Father" and "Son" was dictated more by the requirements of rhythm than by theology. It is intended to relate the cosmic event to the believer personally: "*my* soul", he "freed *me*." This is the good news the singer wants to shout out and share with all of his fellow believers. They are all "chillun" of this same father, who in heaven at "de welcome table" waits also for them, his sons and daughters. The communion of the singing family of God here on earth gives a joyful, liberating foretaste of the unbounded heavenly happiness to come.

17.

Steal Away

Steal away, steal away,
Steal away to Jesus;
Steal away, steal away home,
I ain't got long to stay here.

1.
My Lord, he calls me,
He calls me by the thunder;
The trumpet sounds within-a my soul,
I ain't got long to stay here.

2.
Green trees a-bending,
Poor sinner stands a-trembling; . . .

3.
Tombstones are bursting,
Poor sinner stands a-trembling; . . .

4.
My Lord, he calls me,
He calls me by the lightning; . . .

The soothing chorus, "Steal away, steal away, steal away to Jesus" has strengthened many believers all over the world in extremely difficult situations. How come? Inner migration? Regression? Escape? Yes and no. Intolerable suffering becomes tolerable when the end is in sight or when something beautiful transforms ugliness. A torturer loses his absolute power when the tortured appeals to the one who is Lord also over the torturer. Stealing away to Jesus offers a psychological "out" where no physical "out" is possible. Such a spiritual "out" is healthier than self-destructive despair, bitterness, or hatred. It heals in the midst of hurts and maintains an ultimate hope in the face of earthly hopelessness.

The song was also used as a code message to signal a physical "out" for the slaves. Especially during the time of the Abolitionist movement, when even religious meetings and Bible reading were forbidden, "Steal Away" informed the initiated that a secret meeting was going to be held, or that guides to the free North along the "underground railroad" would soon arrive and that the slaves hadn't "got long to

stay here" any more. It is even plausible that the unsuspect-
ing overseer would be relieved to hear his slaves singing: it
seemed as if his workers had religion on their minds again
as they went about the fields singing and humming their
spirituals. Little did he realize what secret messages were
being conveyed from row to row.

Such code systems seem to develop and work effectively
wherever freedom of speech and information is impaired or
denied. Common expressions and stories are used, but with
a hidden meaning which only the few insiders can decode.
The oppressors, who might have been suspicious of any new
song, would pay no attention to the old ones; they couldn't
very well proscribe the harmless familiar stories, songs, and
symbols of the past, especially those from the common religious heritage. The community of believers has made skill-
ful use of this communication device in situations of persecution down through the ages.

A Dutch Jewess at a conference on Black literature told us
that the humming of "Steal Away" was the code which
helped 200 women in the barracks of a German concentra-
tion camp preserve their "soul" while their bodies were sub-
mitted to a brutal process ending in annihilation. Jesus, a
Jew, had suffered through human brutality. "My Lord, he
calls me" was a command superior to that of any mortal
commander. They could follow his lead toward life in spite
of death.

The Book of Revelation is just such a communication device. It was written to console the early Christians in their
most terrible persecution under the Roman Emperor Domi-
tian, and has been used that way many times since. Numerous symbols which John, the seer, described in his visions
revealed to the insiders of his time that the days of the
persecutors were numbered and that the seemingly victorious
purveyors of violence would be the eternal losers before
God's judgment seat. Ultimately what counts is not power
politics, but love and righteousness.

In early Christian history the most famous of all secret

codes was the sign of the fish. In Greek, each letter of the word for fish—*ichthus*—stood for a word in the confession, "Jesus Christ, God's Son, Savior." When the figure of a fish was drawn in sand or dirt, it symbolized the believer's Lord. Frequently it also signalled a meeting in the catacombs, where Christians had to meet secretly because they were forbidden to meet publicly. In the Roman world of that time Christian use of the fish symbol did not arouse suspicion because the same symbol had been used in one of the legally accepted Syrian religions.

When the persecution is over, such vital symbols often become decorative helps to piety, though they can also be reused as codes when necessary. "Steal Away" was a religious song which gained a political meaning, yet without losing its spiritual dimension. It lives and enriches the worship of believers whether or not they are being persecuted.

Preachers in the South, especially during the early nineteenth century, used to shake people up by frightening them with the terrors of an impending Judgment Day and luring them with sweet promises of heaven from the Book of Revelation. All the imagination which nowadays goes into horror movies and doomsday science fiction went at that time into embellishing the relatively sparse biblical references to the devil, hell, and God's final destruction of this world. Some religious groups predicted the end of the world at specific dates and their followers waited on their mountain tops, robed in white and all ready to be the first to perceive the returning Christ. It is only natural that the slaves shared in these common spectacular visions. Sinners, whether master or slave, feared and trembled, for they would all have to stand and give account of themselves before God's judgment. Believers, however, whether master or slave, would have nothing to fear; they could look forward to the fulfillment of God's promises.

"Steal Away" was originally one of many such songs dealing with the end of time. The lyrics clearly refer to a vision like that of Revelation 8:5–7:

And there were voices, and thunderings, and lightnings, and
an earthquake. And the seven angels which had the seven
trumpets prepared themselves to sound. The first angel
sounded, and there followed hail and fire mingled with
blood, and they were cast upon the earth: and the third part
of trees was burnt up, and all green grass was burnt up.

It is interesting to see how the singer related the apocalyptic
drama to himself. He is not frightened by thunder and
lightning, which in the biblical passage are sent as a plague
to destroy the earth, for he perceives in them God's voice;
they are only a medium whereby his Lord calls him. How
important he must be in God's eyes if the Almighty uses these
powerfully destructive elements just to serve him, just to
beckon him home.

The singer cannot wait for that great Day of the Lord, for
that trumpet which will signal its beginning, when the living
believers will be called first and then the dead will rise from
their graves, when the "tombstones are bursting." Instead,
the singer hears the trumpet sound already "within-a my
soul," signaling the start of the final drama he has so
anxiously awaited. Sinners may have to tremble, but the
believer goes gladly home.

Concerning the end of time Jesus is reported to have said
that then the sinners will "say to the mountains, Fall on us;
and to the hills, Cover us. For if they do these things in a
green tree, what shall be done in the dry?" (Luke 23:30–
31). Many other spirituals visualize the sinners running to
the rocks, seeking in vain for a hiding place. "Steal Away"
takes up the image of the "green trees" as a symbol for the
strong and boasting human whose haughty pride is pathetic
when whipped and lashed by a truly mighty storm.

"Poor" is the adjective frequently used for sinners in the
context of the Judgment; the term suggests sorrow and pity
for those who have gambled their chance away. One might
have expected instead a note of triumphant revenge—that
would have been understandable—but the singer voices only
compassion. "Poor sinners" are likened to the "green trees"

who once stood tall, healthy, proud, and strong, but who are now bending under the lash of greater powers while the believers stride fearlessly home.

It is no wonder that such a song of faith has upheld countless believers in their moments of extremity. Whether in cosmic catastrophes or in personal crises, it could sustain and strengthen the faithful who would "steal away to Jesus . . . home."

18.

Sit Down

1.
t down, servant; sit down, servant;
t down and rest a little while.
t down, servant; sit down, servant;
t down and rest a little while.

2.
know you are tired; sit down, servant . . .

3.
ou come over mountain; sit down, servant . . .

4.
know you had trouble; sit down, servant . . .

5.
I know you been crying; sit down, servant . .

6.
I know you been praying; sit down, servant .

7.
I know you been afflicted; sit down, servant .

8.
It a tiresome journey; sit down, servant . . .

9.
It a long long journey; sit down, servant . . .

Ever since Jesus first told it, the parable of the lost son (Luke 15:11–32) has provided a model for many a Christian's dreams and wishes about home and heaven. The father's reception of the wayward child surpasses anything the prodigal could possibly have imagined. The spirit of that reception speaks in this spiritual as in many other hymns and songs. However, there is a characteristic difference between the spirituals on the one hand and most hymns in most hymnals on the other in the way they talk about heaven. Most church hymns contain comparatives, such as "like," and they talk in the future tense showing some awareness of the difference between the "here and now" and the "beyond and later." Most spirituals, by contrast, talk in the present tense and hardly ever use the comparison formula "like."

The spirituals about heaven report a present reality. Jesus' invitation, "Come unto me, all ye that labor and are heavy laden, and I will give you rest" (Matt. 11:28), is a present consolation needed right now by a tired, worn-out, exhausted worker. "Sit down, servant; I know you are tired; sit down and rest a little while" or "Sit down, chile, sit down" is as earthly and real as the language Jesus used in his stories about heaven. We hear the concerned heavenly father speaking directly to us. He knows that his children have "come a long way and de road is dark," that they "had hard trials." He understands, and beams with loving pride and happiness that his children have made it home from their day/life of hard work. He doesn't scold, or express disappointment but simply accepts and cares like a loving mother or father.

We could hardly imagine an employer, much less a master, speaking in such a warm and wonderfully concerned way with his employee, much less with a slave. But exactly the same words of tender loving care and acceptance are used, whether the version is "Sit down, servant," or "Sit down, child," or "Sit down, sister." Only people who have themselves experienced such human love and concern could possibly visualize such a consoling and relaxing welcome in heaven. God is surely not portrayed as a capricious or brutal master, the stern judge of the world, the commanding patriarch, or even the distant father-king whose name is hallowed in various hymn traditions. In the spirituals God is pictured more in the terms of Isaiah: "As one whom his mother comforteth, so will I comfort you" (Isa. 66:13).

It is not surprising that songs like this came to be used with new meaning and fresh intensity when people who call themselves Christians—people who on Sundays in church sing with gusto from their hymnals, "Help us to make the earth like heaven above"—refused to let a "tired servant," a "sister" or "brother" in Christ, sit down on a park bench or in a bus or in a restaurant. The time had arrived when bad situations, which had become unjustifiable and intolerable, had to be changed here on earth. Interestingly enough, quite a few songs which in the past had successfully functioned to make unchangeable situations tolerable in a Christian fashion *now* facilitated change in a Christian fashion despite unchristian acts of hate, born of insecurity and devilish fear.

As Luther's "A Mighty Fortress Is Our God" has been used in many a battle since the Reformation, so a number of spirituals became effective battle hymns of faith: "Sit down, chile" for the sit-ins at restaurants; "I have a right to the tree of life" for the integration of public parks; "Get on board, little children . . . the gospel train is coming" for the use of train and bus seats whether in back or up front. Later, when the emergency situation is solved with the help of these faith-ful songs, they again sink back down into the repertoire of "normal" everyday church use until another emergency arises. Whenever the spirit of hate and destruction seems to triumph, the songs of faith again perform their corrective, encouraging, reconciling function.

Songs are in some ways like chairs. A chair is the most wonderful thing in the world when "you have come a long way" and are dead-tired and you meet someone who, loving you, does not chase you away like all the others but invites you instead to "sit down and rest." At other times you take chairs for granted; when you are tired of sitting they are even in your way. There are ornate chairs and simple chairs, and different people use them for different purposes. But even if a chair has been in the attic for years, or has been used more for standing on than for sitting, it still is a chair capable of one day serving its original purpose again. The same is true for many a hymn and spiritual. For a while they may be forgotten, or used for a strange or unintended purpose, whether proper or improper (as in a parody). No matter; a good, solid, sturdy song of faith can survive an awful lot of wear and tear—or neglect—and continue to help believers of a later generation survive in a Christian fashion even the most severe difficulties.

19.

Deep River

Deep river, my home is over Jordan;
Deep river, Lord,
I want to cross over into campground,
Lord, I want to cross over into campground,
Lord, I want to cross over into campground,
Lord, I want to cross over into campground.

Oh chillun,
Oh, don't you want to go to that gospel feast,
That promised land, where all is peace?
Walk into heaven and take my seat,
And cast my crown at Jesus' feet;
Lord, I want to cross over into campground,
Lord, I want to cross over into campground,
Lord, I want to cross over into campground.

Deep river, my home is over Jordan;
Deep river, Lord,
I want to cross over into campground.

The melodic mood of this spiritual reminds us of another popular song, "Old Man River." Perhaps both were inspired by the Mississippi. All kinds of myths and legends about rivers come to mind—and have indeed been projected all too eagerly and quickly into the interpretation of "Deep River." The spiritual does not personify the awesome stream as an "old man." Nor does it allegorize human life as a river starting from tiny beginnings, constantly increasing in size and strength, and running along in time through rougher and smoother stretches until it pours itself out, at death, into God's all-encompassing sea of love. Such mystical interpretations are foreign to the world of the spirituals. Equally foreign to them is Heraclitus's concern about the transiency of all that exists. The Greek philosopher held that there is nothing lasting in life: "All is in flux," and "You cannot step into the same river twice"; change is the only constant.

The spiritual reflects a quite different philosophy of life. The only change the singer is interested in is the radical change from the tentative and preliminary life here on earth to the true and enduring life here on earth which also has its reward in heaven. The stream as such is of no interest, except as a marker of the border. The deep river is a constant, difficult barrier between our desert pilgrimage here and the fulfillment of all desires in the "promised land." "Promised land," as we have seen, could have double meaning: usually it meant heaven, but when used in a code song it meant freedom in the North.

Through most of human history the crossing of a mighty river was a major problem. The singer reminds the Lord of this tremendous obstacle, and of his desire to "cross over." Many spirituals celebrate how the Lord helped Moses, Joshua, and Elijah to "cross over," and they express the belief that he will surely do so again.

Roland Hayes was confronted with still another misinterpretation after he sang "Deep River" at a concert in Moscow many years ago. A lady approached him and said in broken English: "I just *know* you were singing about God." Hayes nodded affirmatively and asked why she had doubted it. She replied by telling him the officially given explanation: capitalists would never allow poor working people to share in a picnic on the other side of the river. Officially "Deep River" was interpreted as an early protest song, sung when the slaves felt like walking in on the masters and casting down their hats in defiance. Hayes's anecdote beautifully illustrates how people can read into a text what they want it to say. Such misinterpretations arise when people do not take seriously the text itself, or are unfamiliar with the then common biblical knowledge. For ideological reasons the Moscow interpreters chose not to look up the Bible verse clearly alluded to in the spiritual: "The four and twenty elders fall down before him that sat on the throne, and worship him that liveth for ever and ever, and *cast their crowns before the throne,* saying, Thou art worthy, O Lord, to receive glory and honor and power" (Rev. 4:10–11).

They were obviously not familiar either with the favorite American hymn "Holy, holy, holy!" which uses in the second verse the same biblical image: "All the saints adore thee, / *Casting down their* golden *crowns* around the glassy sea; / Cherubim and seraphim falling down before thee . . ."

The spiritual singer is sure that he will belong to the elders or saints which are mentioned also in other spirituals. He believes that he will have his "seat" among them, and he identifies "him that sat on the throne" with Jesus. In plain, everyday language the vision can be expressed as "cast my crown at Jesus' feet," using "feet" for "throne" because it rhymes with "seat." The "crown" and the "robe" are very dear to the singers, as so many spirituals testify. Taking off the crown is an act not of defiance but of adoration, honoring the host of the "gospel feast."

Once the obstacle of the deep river is overcome there will be no more hindrances. "There is nobody there to turn me out," assures another song. Here the singer asserts: "Walk into heaven and take my seat!" For believers who were used to being excluded from the festivities, who normally led others into beautiful homes and seated them at banquets they had themselves prepared, it is a glorious promise and prospect to be invited in and to be given a seat at the heavenly banquet where everything has been prepared for the wedding feast of the son.

As we have seen, people take the most beautiful, uplifting experiences of their lives and project them into their ideas and visions of heaven, where everything will be bigger and better, indeed perfect. The slaves in the South knew nothing of royal or liturgical splendor. In the Old South the most uplifting experience for all the common people, black and white, workers and overseers, was the camp meeting, which was held for several days after the harvest. People from all over the area would assemble in a designated "campground" for recreation in the widest sense of the word. It was *the* event of the year. Everyone looked forward to these days of revival and festivity after having worked so hard in their isolated fields. Naturally believers tried to visualize an indescribable heaven in terms of this most joyful earthly experience. It was precisely because the slaves had been allowed to take part in these "picnics," and had enjoyed the sharing and singing so much, that they could envision heaven as a super "gospel feast" in the "campground" across Jordan, the heavenly "promised land." There would be "no partin' " any more, as another song consoles. All would finally be together at "home" and at rest.

20.

In Dat Great Gittin'-Up Mornin'

1.
I'm a-gwine tell you 'bout de comin'
 ob de Savior,
Fare you well, fare you well;
I'm a-gwine tell you 'bout de comin'
 ob de Savior,
Fare you well, fare you well.

2.
Dar's a better day a-comin', . . .

3.
When my Lord speaks to his fadder, . . .

4.
Says, Fadder, I'm tired o'bearin', . . .

5.
Tired o' bearin' for poor sinners. . . .

6.
Oh, preachers, fold your Bibles, . . .

7.
Pray'r-makers, pray no more; . . .

8.
For de last soul's converted. . . .

In dat great gittin'-up mornin',
Fare you well, fare you well;
In dat great gittin'-up mornin',
Fare you well, fare you well.

9.
De Lord spoke to Gabriel: . . .

10.
Say, go look behind de altar, . . .

11.
Take down de silver trumpet, . . .

12.
Go down to de seaside, . . .

13.
Place one foot on de dry land, . . .

14.
Place de oder on de sea, . . .

15.
Raise your hand to heaven, . . .

16.
Declare by your Maker . . .

17.
Dat time shall be no longer. . . .

In dat great gittin'-up mornin', . . .

18.
Blow your trumpet, Gabriel. . . .

19.
Lord, how loud shall I blow it? . . .

20.
Blow it right calm and easy, . . .

21.
Do not alarm my people; . . .

22.
Tell dem to come to Judgment. . . .

In dat great gittin'-up mornin', . . .

23.
Den you see de coffins bustin', . . .

24.
Den you see de Christians risin'; . . .

25.
Den you see de righteous marchin', . . .

26.
Dey are marchin' home to heaven. . . .

27.
Den look upon Mount Zion; . . .

28.
You see my Jesus comin' . . .

29.
Wid all his holy angels. . . .

30.
Where you runnin', sinner? . . .

31.
Judgment day is comin'. . . .

In dat great gittin'-up mornin', . . .

32.
Gabriel, blow your trumpet. . . .

33.
Lord, how loud shall I blow it? . . .

34.
Loud as seven peals of thunder! . . .

35.
Wake de sleepin' nations! . . .

36.
Den you see poor sinners risin', . . .

37.
See de dry bones a-creepin'. . . .

In dat great gittin'-up mornin' . . .

38.
Den you see de world on fire, . . .

39.
You see de moon a-bleedin', . . .

40.
See de stars a-fallin', . . .

41.
See de elements meltin', . . .

42.
See de forked lightnin', . . .

43.
Hear de rumblin' thunder; . . .

44.
Earth shall reel and totter, . . .

45.
Hell shall be uncapped, . . .

46.
De dragon shall be loosened. . . .

47.
Fare you well, poor sinner. . . .

In dat great gittin'-up mornin', . . .

48.
Den you look up in de heaven, . . .

49.
See your mother in heaven, . . .

50.
While you're doomed to destruction. . . .

51.
When de partin' word is given, . . .

52.
De Christian shouts to your ruin: . . .

53.
No mercy'll ever reach you. . . .

In dat great gittin'-up mornin', . . .

54.
Den you'll cry out for cold water, . . .

55.
While de Christians shoutin' in glory, . .

56.
Sayin' amen to your damnation. . . .

57.
Den you hear de sinner sayin', . . .

58.
Down I'm rollin, down I'm rollin'. . . .

59.
Den de righteous housed in heaven . . .

60.
Live wid God forever. . . .

In dat great gittin'-up mornin'. . . .

Jonathan Edwards's famous sermon, "Sinners in the Hands of an Angry God" (1741), has its equivalent in the Negro song-sermon "In Dat Great Gittin'-up Mornin'," made famous by James Weldon Johnson. Sinners responded to the great New England revival preacher as children respond to a modern horror movie, with moans and cries and shrieks. Many were scared to death as they visualized themselves dangling over hell-fire, ready at any minute to plunge down into the bottomless pit. The preacher had warned them that all their prestige and righteousness would have no more power to keep them "out of hell than a spider's web would have to stop a fallen rock." People were frightened into accepting Christ as the only rescue from the wrath of an angry God who could drop them at any time into the most horrible torment.

Hieronymus Bosch, Leonardo da Vinci, and many less famous European painters had visualized the twisted, tormented bodies. In gory detail they showed the sadistic devils who were burning, piercing, beating, and cutting the poor sinners eternally in hell—but also the unrepentant sinners on earth who were martyring the saints with equally horrendous tortures. Western art and literature—think of Dante's *Inferno*—have been obsessed with portraying all kinds of "cruel and unusual punishment" both on and under the earth.

It is impressive by way of contrast to observe that the slaves, who suffered no less for the sake of the Southern economy than earlier Christians had for the sake of their faith, sang hardly at all about the torments of hell. It would have been very understandable indeed had they wished severe punishment on the brutal, unrepentant sinners who had made their lives so hard and miserable here on earth. Old Testament texts offered ample material for seeking unbridled revenge for what the "enemies of God" had done to a believer. The spirituals, however, are born of the Christ-spirit: "love your enemies" and "Father forgive them." They ignore passages of revenge to an amazing degree.

Instead of resorting to the pending torments of hell, the

spirituals employ natural catastrophies to frighten sinners into repentance. In the South, as in the African homelands, people were often helplessly exposed to the elements. Stars and moon were the only guides on a dark night not yet lit by car and street lights. Many a person could escape from an evil neighbor or boss into the wilderness. But if the stars should fall or the moon turn to blood, there would be no orientation in the dark, no escape; horrendous panic would overcome the utterly helpless creatures seeking shelter and refuge.

For this reason images mentioned in stanzas 38–44 of this long ballad, "de world on fire" (2 Pet. 3:10), "de moon a-bleedin' " (Rev. 6:12), "de stars a-fallin' " (Rev. 6:13), "de elements meltin'," "thunder and lightnin'" (Rev. 8:5), "Earth shall reel and totter" (Joel 2:10) are found in many spirituals. These frightening events are mentioned, how-ever, mostly from the perspective of the believers who, be-cause they have accepted Christ, won't have to fear them. They are mentioned as an invitation to others to come into the heavenly shelter too.

There is pity and sadness but hardly sadistic joy in the doom "to destruction when de partin' word is given" (50, 51). The closest the singer comes to voicing vengeful satisfaction over any "poor sinner" are the lines "de Christian shouts to your ruin: / No mercy'll ever reach you" (52, 53), verses which simply paraphrase the end of Jesus' parable about the rich man in hell who sees Lazarus in heaven and cries:

> Father Abraham, have mercy on me, and send Lazarus, that he may dip the tip of his finger in water, and cool my tongue; for I am tormented in this flame. But Abraham said, Son, remember that thou in thy lifetime receivedst thy good things, and likewise Lazarus evil things: but now he is com-forted, and thou art tormented. And beside all this, between us and you there is a great gulf fixed; so that they which would pass from hence to you cannot. (Luke 16:24–26)

In the course of church history people have latched onto the concept of compensatory justice, which can be simply summarized: *We* had poor conditions here on earth; therefore we are going to have glorious conditions in heaven; *you,* however, had a comfortable life on earth; therefore it will serve you right to be miserable in hell. Interestingly enough, the spirituals don't mention this type of reasoning. For them the great divide is not based on income. It is not a case of rich versus poor, but of the righteous versus the sinners, the rich in faith versus the "poor sinners" who, having excluded themselves from the blessed "chillun of God," will be left behind in a state of terrible want: "Den you'll cry out for cold water" (54). Several spirituals mention this cry for water as an expression of torment. Beyond that "great gulf" mercy will not be able to reach poor sinners any more. Jonathan Edwards's description of the slippery slope on which terrified sinners try vainly to keep from sliding and rolling down into hell is echoed in the final scene: "Den you hear de sinner sayin', / Down I'm rollin', down I'm rollin'" (57–58) while "De righteous housed in heaven / Live wid God forever" (59–60).

The Old Testament prophet of the exile had written about a "suffering servant" whom the New Testament writers identified with Jesus: "Surely he hath borne our griefs and carried our sorrows" (Isa. 53:4). The suffering, serving slaves identified deeply with Jesus, feeling that even *his* tolerance must finally run out: Someday "my Lord" will say to "his fadder," "Fadder, I'm tired o' bearin' for poor sinners" (4, 5). "Poor sinners" is, as we have seen, a standard phrase, one of the many "pre-fab" units; it contains not so much impatience, anger, or fury with these awful people who never learn, but pity and mercy toward those creatures that have loaded so much sin on him.

The singer tells the preachers and prayer-makers to quit their work too, because their job is now done: "de last soul's converted" (8). The phrase is a result of the long and interesting development of an ancient Jewish concept about the coming of the kingdom. It was believed that the Messiah and God's kingdom would come if only the Sabbath was kept

perfectly, even once. Jesus did not share this expectation.
The Gospels report several examples of how Jesus broke the
sabbath laws in order to help people in need and how he was
challenged for doing so. "The sabbath," he replied, "was
made for man, and not man for the sabbath" (Mark 2:27).
Since Jesus' followers acknowledged him as the expected
Messiah, the former precondition for the coming of the kingdom was revised: "This gospel of the kingdom shall be
preached in all the world for a witness unto all nations; and
then shall the end come" (Matt. 24:14). Many centuries of
preaching followed. The "good news" did reach many
nations, but history also witnessed perversions of the gospel
message. The issue came up again during the Reformation,
which held that perfection of ritual alone was not enough.
Luther, as well as the Bible translators commissioned by King
James, translated Jesus' parting command to his disciples
according to Matthew 28:19: "Go ye therefore [into all the
world] and *teach* all nations, baptizing them . . ." Accordingly, Luther defined "church" as coming into being where
the word is preached and the sacraments are administered
properly. Calvin, the second generation reformer whose
theology influenced American Puritanism more strongly,
added the educational concern that the word had to be not
only preached but understood. Many free churches in America stiffened the requirement even more to include the "conversion of every soul" or, as the recent Revised Standard
Version of the Bible translates the famous command: "make
disciples of all nations, baptizing them . . ."—a notion which
has fueled missionary zeal at home and abroad. In its vision
of "dat great gittin'-up mornin' " our song-sermon declares
that this basic requirement has finally been fulfilled: "de last
soul's converted" (8). No more prayers have to be made
(7), for everything is now ready for the Savior to come.

The singer identifies the angel in John's vision—"I saw
another mighty angel come down from heaven" (Rev. 10:1)
—as Gabriel. He visualizes first how Gabriel received his
instruction from God in a very human, casual way. The

Almighty speaks to the archangel as an informal preacher might talk to an elder friend: "Say, go look behind de altar, / Take down de silver trumpet." (10–11). The seer of Revelation was awe-stricken by the appearance of the gigantic angel and describes reverently and ceremoniously what he observed in his vision:

> And he set his right foot upon the sea, and his left foot on the earth. . . . And the angel which I saw stand upon the sea and upon the earth lifted up his hand to heaven, and sware by him that liveth for ever and ever, who created heaven, and the things that therein are, and the earth, and the things that therein are, and the sea, and the things which are therein, that there should be time no longer.
>
> (Rev. 10:2, 5, 6)

The song-sermon concentrates this long, solemn description of the event into a few simple instructions which can easily be followed step by step: "Go down to de seaside, / Place one foot on de dry land, / Place de oder on de sea, / Raise your hand to heaven, / Declare by your Maker / Dat time shall be no longer" (12–17).

Then follows a charming dialogue between the concerned Lord and his conscientious servant about how the trumpet should be blown. The Lord is obviously a good trumpet player: "Blow it right calm and easy" (20), for "the dead in Christ shall rise first" (I Thess. 4:16) and they do not deserve to be "alarmed" (21) as the "poor sinners" will be when the trumpet blows "loud as seven peals of thunder" (34). John heard that "seven thunders uttered their voices" (Rev. 10:3) before the angel declared the end of time, but the singer-preacher makes it God's instruction on volume for the trumpeter—how to really shake up "de sleepin' nations" (35).

The reaction of the dead corresponds to the precise trumpet calls: The righteous march victoriously into heaven (24–26). We are reminded of the jubilant, triumphant song "When De Saints Come Marchin' In." But the poor sinners don't even dare to stand up. Ezekiel's fantastically hopeful vision of the valley with the dry bones which shall come to life again when the children of Israel return from the Babylonian captivity (Ezek. 37:1–14) is used here to describe the humiliated, hopeless sinners who are creeping along (37) like a dog with a bad conscience begging for mercy at its master's feet.

The thrust of the whole song-sermon is to shake up the sinners, whether rich or poor, black or white, so that all might repent before they hear the fateful words, as some spirituals put it: "too late, sinner!" If the warning call is heard there should be no final departing, no separation—no "fare you well," as the refrain drums relentlessly into the consciousness of all.

The song-sermon concludes with the promise "Den de righteous housed in heaven / Live wid God forever" (59, 60), a reformulation of the beloved quotation from John 14:2–3: "In my Father's house are many mansions: . . . And if I go and prepare a place for you, I will come again, and receive you unto myself; that where I am, there ye may be also." These last two stanzas are the fulfillment of stanzas 27–29: "Den look upon Mount Zion; / You see my Jesus comin' / Wid all his holy angels." The song is rounded out with this beatific vision of a permanent home in the new heaven, visualized in the most beautified earthly terms.

21.

When De Saints Come Marchin' In

When de saints come marchin' in,
When de saints come marchin' in,
Lord, I want to be in dat number
When de saints come marchin' in.

1.
I have a lovin' brother.
He is gone on before.
An' I promised I would meet him
When dey crown Him Lord of all.

When dey crown Him Lord of all,
When dey crown Him Lord of all,
Lord, I want to be in dat number
When dey crown Him Lord of all.

2.
I have a lovin' sister.
She is gone on before.
An' I promised I would meet her
When dey gather roun' de throne.

When dey gather roun' de throne,
When dey gather roun' de throne,
Lord, I want to be in dat number
When dey gather roun' de throne.

Louis Armstrong and the record industry have made "When De Saints Come Marchin' In" probably the most widely known spiritual in the world. His "trumpet sounds within-a our soul" as it were, and people vibrate to the sweeping rhythm whether at a New Orleans funeral or a Paris dance. Few people any more, however, understand the spiritual dimension of the song, that it refers to the end of time, when the angels' trumpets are to give the signal to "gather together his elect from the four winds, from one end of heaven to the other" (Matt. 24:31). John the seer reports of his vision: "And I heard the number of them which were sealed: and there were sealed a hundred and forty and four thousand of all the tribes of the children of Israel. . . . After this I beheld, and lo, a great multitude, which no man could number, of all nations, and kindreds, and people, and tongues, stood before the throne, and before the Lamb, clothed with white robes" (Rev. 7:4, 9).

One spiritual reversed the order, starting with the general and then getting more specific:

> 1.
> John saw de number, dat no man could number (3x)
>   Comin' up comin' up on high.
>
> 2.
> John saw de hundred and forty-four thousand (3x)
>   Comin' up comin' up on high.
>
> 3.
> Tell John not to call de roll till I get dere (3x)
>   Sinner man you better believe.

The singer wants the "sinner" to get converted so that he too will be "in dat number." Several spirituals mention a roll call—which field slaves experienced daily—as the time when the decision would be made whether a person would be in the number of believers going to heaven or be marked for exclusion and punishment with the sinners. Those who could not decide, or decided tardily, to leave their life of sin behind would hear the "too late, sinner" which Noah spoke to those who came running to the ark only after the rain had started falling: "Too late, Massa Jesus lock de door, / Take de key to heben wid him," or using an image found in other spirituals: "Too late, de train done gone."

There is an acute sense of urgency. The believers want to register in time. "Lord, I want to be in dat number"—so as not to be left out of the most important spectacle of history: "when de saints come marchin' in . . . when dey crown him Lord of all . . . when dey gather roun' de throne." Believers who have held to Jesus, who have proven during their lifetime that they belong to the "sainthood of all believers," want to make sure that they participate in his inauguration by marching in that solemn procession of all the saints.

The first stanza names also a very personal reason for the urgent desire to go to heaven: "I have a lovin' brother. / He is gone on before. / An' I promised I would meet him." The second stanza names a "lovin' sister," and the song is easily extended to include other faith- or blood-related members of the family of God.   The promise at the deathbed to follow the dying loved one on the road of faith to heaven imposed a strong obligation on the living.   It reinforced the personal desire—whether for reasons of curiosity, excitement, or honor—to share in the most significant and spectacular event of history that would also end history.

All earthly structures of separation and distinction, of inferiority and superiority, become irrelevant, they lose their deadly seriousness, when viewed under the perspective of such a marvelous future.   Patterns of discrimination, which hurt or cripple in this life as severely as deafness and lameness, do not disqualify one for membership in God's people, as another version asserts: "I may be lame and I cannot walk, / I'll be one in that number, / When the saints march in."

"When De Saints Come Marchin' In" is a triumphant entry song.   It simulates the glorious entry into heaven at Christ's inauguration as Lord of all lords, when peace will rule forever.   The song vibrates with the assurance of faith.   This dimension is often lost, however, when people today merely rush to the dance floor at the sound of the band's trumpet in order to be in the number of those who will strut around in a parade for a few minutes of musical excitement.

22.

Heav'n, Heav'n, Heav'n

Heav'n, heav'n, heav'n,
Ev'rybody talkin' 'bout heav'n ain't goin' dere;
Heav'n, heav'n,
I'm goin' to shout all ovah God's heav'n.

1.
I got a robe, you got a robe,
All o' God's chillun got a robe;
When I get to heav'n goin' to put on my robe,
I'm goin' to shout all ovah God's heav'n.

2.
I got-a wings, you got-a wings,
All o' God's chillun got-a wings;
When I get to heav'n goin' to put on my wings,
I'm goin' to fly all ovah God's heav'n.

3.
I got a harp, you got a harp,
All o' God's chillun got a harp;
When I get to heav'n goin' to take up my harp,
I'm goin' to play all ovah God's heav'n.

4.
I got-a shoes, you got-a shoes,
All o' God's chillun got-a shoes;
When I get to heav'n goin' to put on my shoes,
I'm goin' to walk all ovah God's heav'n.

5.
I got a song, you got a song,
All o' God's chillun got a song;
When I get to heav'n goin' to sing a new song,
I'm goin' to sing all ovah God's heav'n.

6.
I got a cross, you got a cross,
All o' God's chillun got a cross;
When I get to heav'n goin' to lay down my cross,
I'm goin' to shout all ovah God's heav'n.

Astronauts describing their experiences on the moon use American English, our earth language. However much we may yearn for a beyond, whether we like it or not, we are still earthlings. When the astronauts tried to help us see and feel what they were seeing and feeling out there in space, they used over and over again the little word "like." They drew comparisons—from desert country in the West, from volcano territory, from summer and winter, from deep sea diving, and from many other fields of human experience— all in order to help us imagine a place none of us had ever been before. Television simulated many of the moments it could not cover directly. Yet we knew that for all the pictures and descriptions we could never fully imagine what it would be "like" as long as we hadn't been there ourselves.

For the first time in history, though, someone was reporting to millions of people on something beyond all earthly experience. It was like when the rich man in hell asked Abraham in heaven to send someone back to earth to tell his brothers (Luke 16:27–28). The astronauts' reports have even changed our perceptions of life here on earth.

But a fellow earthling is yet to come who can give us an eyewitness report of how it is in hell or in heaven. Jesus did not say much about the hereafter. On this subject earthlings remain dependent on their "like" projections.

Early Christians, who had experienced the temple cult and appearances of the emperor as the most spectacular events in their lives, often envisioned comparable but even more spectacular pageants for heaven. They speculated about unending celebrations and solemn processions, with choirs in white robes singing even more beautiful new songs, accompanied by better orchestras of trumpets, cymbals, and harps. Imagery in the Book of Revelation alludes to a splendor more pompous than even a Roman emperor could display. It also projects into the heavenly Jerusalem the most magnificent purification ritual and sacrifice imaginable, comparable to but even exceeding that performed by hierarchies of priests at the festive cultic events in the Jerusalem temple.

Life in colonial America was vastly different from that of
first-century Jerusalem. Life was unspectacular and hard
for most people, especially for the slaves. It is only natural
in such circumstances that hopeful believers selected images
from the Bible that related comfortingly to their needs.
Camp-meeting songs and Negro spirituals alike sung frequently about "rest" at "home up in the heavens" where the
righteous will enjoy their "shoes," "robe," "harp," and "milk
an' honey." The "heavenly feast" would mean reunion with
loved ones, with Jesus and the angels, and with such faith-
relatives as Peter, Paul, Daniel, Moses, Mary, and John.

Thus, verses such as "I got a robe" or "I got-a shoes" are
far from egotistical bragging of the type: "Look what I've
got and you don't have!" On the contrary, believers *share*
their joy: "I got . . . you got / All o' God's chillun got."
There are no underprivileged "poor raggedies" among the
children of God. There is plenty for all—no worrying, no
grabbing, no "first come, first served" out of a limited supply.
The robe, the shoes, the harp, and all the other heavenly
goods are waiting for the faithful child to use. The imagery
is reminiscent of Jesus' parable of the lost son, in which the
father—usually understood as signifying God—said "Bring
forth the best robe, and put it on him" (Luke 15:22). After
performing the most degrading task a Jew could do, that of
feeding pigs for foreigners, the son on reaching home was
given not only a robe but also a ring and shoes—status symbols indicating that he had been fully reinstated as a son
worthy of all honor.

Informal revival songs as well as formal "white" hymns
sang about the "rings and robes and royal sandals" which
believers expect when they enter heaven. It is curious that
the religious songs of the Afro-American slaves, while they
allude to this parable, never mention the ring, even though
rings seem to play a more important role in African cultures
than in most others. Many spirituals delight in the heavenly
"robe" and quite a few mention the "crown," which is
promised in several biblical passages. Also the "shoes," or

"slippers" as they are called in other songs, seem to be a welcome present, but never the ring. One would expect the African slaves to latch on to a promised ring in the religion of the new land as something familiar, homelike. However, many of the preachers who spread Christianity in the Old South at revival and camp meetings preached to all of their listeners the requirement of "total conversion." This meant that all forms of paganism, the so-called life of sin, with all its alluring temptations, had to be left behind. The rings as predominant status symbols of the "old world" seem to have fallen under their ban.

"I'm goin' to shout all ovah God's heaven" is not the expression of an ill-mannered youngster who refuses to quiet down and insists on disturbing the heavenly peace by shouting all over the place. No, this refrain is simply an outburst of unmitigated joy over the unbounded happiness of heaven, a joy which is expressed in the totality of a person's being— in word, sound, and motion.

Three times in succession believers sing the promising word "heav'n"; with each repetition the tune lifts the spirits another step upwards, but then there is the sudden warning that "Ev'rybody talkin' 'bout heav'n ain't goin' dere." The chorus is an adaptation of Jesus' statement, "Not everyone that saith unto me, Lord, Lord, shall enter into the kingdom of heaven; but he that doeth the will of my Father which is in heaven" (Matt. 7:21). The Israelites of old were very concerned about possible misuse of God's name, a name which was solemnly protected by their basic constitution: "Thou shalt not take the name of the Lord thy God in vain: for the Lord will not hold him guiltless that taketh his name in vain" (Exod. 20:7). In fear of transgressing this commandment the people of the Old Testament replaced the original "name," the one by which God had revealed himself to Moses, with "Lord." Their awe of the name and fear of violating it was so great that they didn't use it at all, or used circumlocutions or substitutes. Today nobody knows for sure even how to pronounce the Hebrew letters which scholars sometimes refer to as Yahweh, sometimes as Jehovah. Jesus warned the religious "lobbyists" of his day that their constant calling "Lord, Lord" would not make them acceptable; no, decisive rather is the way they carry out God's will.

The singers are less concerned with the abuse of prayer than with the bragging and boasting of those people who talk as if heaven were theirs and not God's. Only with the proper attitude of thankful appreciation can believers continue enumerating their heavenly presents stanza by stanza. There are so many that there is really no limit to the number or possible sequence. The singers, like the psalmists before them, would forever "sing unto the Lord a new song" (Ps. 96:1) until the day of that "new song" (Rev. 14:3) which would perfect and complete the series.

"I got-a wings" may be influenced by the widespread imaginative notion in Christian tradition about all kinds of angels with wings in heaven. The prophet Isaiah used an impressive image of soaring, the most impressive imaginable before airplanes, that of the majestic, powerful eagle, king of the birds, rising above the highest mountain; for him it was an illustration of faith, the new life with God: "They that wait upon the Lord shall renew their strength; they shall mount up with wings as eagles; they shall run, and not be weary; and they shall walk, and not be faint" (Isa. 40:31). In the spiritual the "wings" are yet one more welcome present waiting in heaven for those who have faithfully and untiringly run their course in life; Isaiah's "mount up" is understood as technological vocabulary: "put on my wings."

The last stanza surprises us at first. How can people climax their list of exuberant, exhilarating joy by mentioning "a cross"? Wouldn't a cross instead be something to complain about, to rebel against? Down through the ages people who did not live from the strength of this unusual faith have broken under their various crosses; they got stuck in their predicament. But those who heard and heeded Jesus' invitation, "Whosoever doth not bear his cross, and come after me, cannot be my disciple" (Luke 14:27), did not get "weary" or "faint"—as Isaiah had prophesied—even in extreme circumstances. They were enabled to reinterpret man's extremities as God's opportunities and their hopeless sighing was transformed to hopeful singing.

Thus, this last stanza reminds the singers of present reality, lest they "become so heavenly minded that they are no earthly good." Right here and now "I got a cross." You have a cross too, you and all of God's children. But whatever our specific difficulties, we are not alone; we all partake of the problems as well as of the joys. To be children of God does not mean a problem-free life. It does mean that the community of believers makes it easier for us to bear our troubles, and that we may "lay down" our cross. I may "lay down my burden, down by the riverside," before entering the heavenly "promised land" where we'll "study war no more." Then we shall "put on" the robe and sing because "God shall wipe away all our tears" (Isa. 25:8; Rev. 21:4). Where suffering is eased by a sympathetic and concerned community, and terminated by joy, crosses can become light. This contagious, joyous faith sets energies free to help and heal and strengthen "all o' God's chillun."

23.

He's Got the Whole World
in His Hands

1.

He's got the whole world in his hands,
He's got the big round world in his hands;
He's got the whole world in his hands,
He's got the whole world in his hands.

2.

He's got the wind and the rain in his hands,
He's got the sun and the moon in his hands;
He's got the wind and the rain in his hands,
He's got the whole world in his hands.

3.

He's got the little bitsy baby in his hands,
He's got the tiny little baby in his hands;
He's got the itsy bitsy baby in his hands,
He's got the whole world in his hands.

4.

He's got you and me, brother, in his hands,
He's got you and me, sister, in his hands;
He's got you and me, brother, in his hands,
He's got the whole world in his hands.

5.

He's got everybody in his hands,
He's got everybody in his hands;
He's got everybody in his hands,
He's got the whole world in his hands.

The simplest and yet most profound confession of belonging for people who have been uprooted, shoved, and shipped from one part of the world to another is the statement that God has the whole world in his hand. One would almost think that this song was created in the middle of the twentieth century, which has witnessed a higher number of displaced persons and refugees than ever before in history. But in fact it was created by people who were hardly informed at all about global matters, people who lived in a time before television had brought world politics, glory, and misery into every living room. A song that began in oral tradition has been preserved for our time, a period in which governments and businesses literally reach out with all the sophisticated means at their disposal to get the whole world into *their* hands.

The confession intoned in the spiritual is even more relevant today because of an almost universal fear of the powerful people who are now capable of destroying our whole world with their doomsday weapons—and who just might be tempted to use them. The masters of power everywhere need to hear that it is not they but God who has the whole world in *his* hands. In the recent struggle over white or black power a gospel song affirmed: "He's got all power, / God has all power, / He's got the whole world in his hand." The song vibrates with the same fear-conquering faith which Paul expressed in his Letter to the Romans, which has given courage to uncounted numbers of distressed people throughout history:

> If God be for us, who can be against us? . . . For I am persuaded, that neither death, nor life, nor angels, nor principalities, nor powers, nor things present, nor things to come, Nor height, nor depth, nor any other creature, shall be able to separate us from the love of God, which is in Christ Jesus our Lord.   (Rom. 8:31, 38–39)

The singer spells out what this global confession means in personal terms: "you and me, brother," "you and me, sister," even "the itsy bitsy baby"—they are all in God's hands. Nobody is too little, too insignificant. And there are no foreigners! Everywhere is home. All people in all places are brothers and sisters guarded and guided by God's corrective and protective love. And where all are included, nobody has the right to exclude. This universality, however, implies also that nobody can get away with hate and brutality. Even the enemies, who sometimes seem to be in total control, are ultimately not absolute. They too are in God's power— "everybody."

The fiber of faith expressed in this powerful song enables wholesome survival under any and all circumstances in this beautiful yet brutal world of ours. Believers can take courage from Jesus' assurance that "no man is able to pluck them out of my Father's hand" (John 10:29).

All o' God's Chillun Got a Song

"I got a song, you got a song, / All o' God's chillun got a song," and not only one song but many. Throughout the ages people everywhere have related their happiness and sorrow, their hopes and frustrations, to God in song. In singing they relativize their problems and compound their joys. Since all of God's children are different, their responses to God in song necessarily differ. A pluralistic humankind naturally produces "plurals of hallelujah."

All over the world there has been a tendency to offer the Almighty only "the most beautiful sound," only "the most poetic image." Experts have created and performed sacred music of breath-taking beauty. But there has been a high price for this emphasis on excellence: the average believer has been excluded from active praise and participation and pushed into the ranks of the silent admirers and listeners. The recording and publishing industry today accomplishes the same kind of passivity on the part of the "common people," for it removes the best performers from the ordinary congregation and dictates homogenized, standardized songs.

This specialization means a double loss: the musician is deprived of creative and corrective feedback from the community, and the congregation loses the input from its most talented poets and singers. There is, however, a positive side too: records, sheet music, and tapes have given many songs a world-wide audience. In the process, though, the music has taken on primary and even independent importance while the content of faith is watered down in order to win more buyers.

Negro spirituals are songs of faith by the people, of the people, and for the people. They were created by musically and poetically gifted individuals within a community that lacked all formal education. Everyone in the congregation had both the right and the responsibility to refine and polish a song until the best form was found for expressing the common faith.

The singing of spirituals allowed for individual expression within the shared rhythm of life. The believers' criterion for a "good spiritual" was not whether it met the highest standards of aesthetic beauty worthy of the Supreme Being, but whether it expressed a true feeling, a true response in faith to a loving God who accepts us as we are, where we are. In the words of "Jacob's Ladder," the criterion for all service is: "Sister/Brother, do you love my Jesus? If you love him why not serve him?" Serve him with your whole self, your weaknesses as well as your strengths, your fears as well as your faith. Spirituals were conceived and sung in keeping with the biblical commandment recorded in both Testaments: "Love the Lord thy God with all thy *heart*, and with all thy *soul*, and with all thy *mind*" (Deut. 6:5; Matt. 22:37).

In an age of *heart* transplants, *soul* music, and *mind*-boggling technological advances, God's love must become "flesh" in poetic images and musical idioms different from those of the days before copyright laws and electronic amplifiers. But the great old spirituals and hymns created in former cultures can still inspire us to do with *our* heart, soul, and mind what the ancient psalmists called all of God's children to do in every age and circumstance—"sing unto the Lord a new song."

Index

SCRIPTURAL REFERENCES

NAMES AND SUBJECTS